757 Perspectives
Vol. II: Evolutions

Hampton Roads Poetic Collective

ISBN: 154249740X
ISBN-13: 978-1542497404

DEDICATION

For Faith. For Hope. For those who, sometimes, forget love doesn't hurt.
For the angels who help them remember.

CONTENTS

ACKNOWLEDGMENTS

Many people and stories have shaped this collection. Its true direction was found in the tales of innocence, abuse and, finally, independence and growth that survivors of domestic violence encounter each day. We hope our stories will be your stories and our triumphs will be your triumphs. The work done by Neisha Himes, G.R.O.W. Foundation and countless others has inspired a ragtag group of poets to become something greater than the sum of their parts.

Foreword

The Hampton Roads Artistic Collective and its literary division, the Poetic Collective, is a not-for-profit organization created for and by artists to showcase the talent of our local arts community. Its mission is to provide a medium for artists to see their visions brought to fruition while benefitting a worthy local cause.

For this project, we have chosen to support Girls Recognizing Our Worth (G.R.O.W.) Foundation. Founded in 2016, by fellow poet, activist and advocate Neisha Himes, G.R.O.W. aims to assist victims and survivors of domestic violence with the resources needed to lead a safe and productive life. It is G.R.O.W.'s continued goal to bring awareness to this epidemic while teaching women and children of all ages to recognize and embrace their worth. As a survivor, herself, Neisha uses her story as an inspiration to victims, other survivors and women facing a variety of obstacles to ultimate happiness. We hope, in our small way, to do the same.

This volume attempts to mimic the evolution of a soul. It echoes the path we must all travel to find peace and strength. These collected works will journey from times of innocence, times that try the soul and, ultimately, to times of resurrection and growth.

Thank for your support. Enjoy the ride.

Evolutions

Eden

Evolutions

Sidewalk Confessions
Sarah Eileen Williams

One.
I have a bad habit of counting footsteps.

Two.
To distract myself from the sharp stabs of heels and the pounding of boots,
I tend to make music out of the quiet pattering of children's rainboots
And the tingling of toddlers' sandals.
I find the continual beatings of feet against my surface almost criminal,
But my complaints only lodge themselves within bricks
And my screams get battered into the pavement –
I have a hard job.

Three.
I love insecure people.
Shy souls consistently looking down always grace me with their gaze,
And their attention is comforting.
Confident people overlook me like I'm no more important than the idle chatter
They share with other arrogant strangers as they meander across my surface.
I hate ingratitude.

Four.
I have witnessed how fine the line is between life and death,
Desperation and tragedy.

Five.
I watched you steady yourself far above me,
Gazing hungrily down at my paved curves.
You took one last bravening breath,
Closed your eyes –

And let yourself fall.

Let
Gravity
Hurdle
You to my
Unforgiving surface.

In one split second, I *felt* your soul abandon you,
Your agony spilled over my concrete skin like a messy afterthought.

Six.
I wish I had a voice, a comforting one adept in the art of life saving.
It would affirm your beauty, reassure you
That you would have soon walked on me with a hopeful stride
Replacing the shackled shuffle you had become accustomed to.

Seven.
Because there's no sidewalk deity,
No immortal bricklayer to alleviate my pain once yours has ended.
No street sweeper proficient enough to wipe clean the macabre memories
That rest within my cracked pavement.

Eight.
I'm sorry.

Nine.
I wish I weren't so hard,
So unforgiving.

Ten.
So to distract myself from the threat of new tragedies,

One.
I have a bad habit of counting footsteps.

Identity
Jorge Mendez

None of these faces look familiar.
Neither does the one in the mirror.
Or the store window.
Or the puddle.

One looks like a warden though.
He's holding a clipboard.
I'm not sure what he's writing down
but I hear the pen grinding against the paper.
Sounds like brakes at the last minute.
Like voices in broken homes.

Another smiles like he knows the punchline
to a joke I haven't told.
Laughs late.
He's thin and Talcum.
Grin wider than the width of his jaw line.
He concerns me.
Seems fake.
Yields a false positive.

There's one who keeps his face hidden.
Only shows me the top of his head.
Eyes fixed to the ground.
Admires has feet,
wonders where they'll take him.
He looked up once but couldn't handle the glare.
Keeps his eyes covered these days.

The girl is fragile but fierce.
Blade of grass.
Spring time sharp.
She cries for the one she couldn't love.
Settles for the one that can't love her.
or just didn't.
They say all men have a feminine side.
Mine wears the pants.

The youngest one is my favorite.

Sings out of key.
Doesn't care.
Sings louder.
wears a towel around his neck.
It's where he gets his powers.
Lives in a blanket fort.
The walls are impervious.
He takes me by the hand.
Tucks me behind the sheets and tells me
that as long as I stop growing up I'll be safe here.
He makes Drawings of the rest of us.
Draws me holding a tissue,
Wearing a towel around my neck.

Good Night
C.J. Expression

I'm off to the world behind my eyelids,
where words come in crayon
and giggles chime like bells;
to the place where wingless flight
grants freedom and insight.

There, Moon and I converse for hours,
sipping stardust,
forgetting Yesterday
and Tomorrow,
living only in
Now.

Process
Victoria Cartagena

I am a work in the progress ...
Process ...
Sex?
No, miss me with the mess!
I am a mess ...
Message?
Missed age?
Moments gone
Childhood scared
Developmental damage
Damn age.
I am a process
In process
In due time
Due date
Labor pains
I am a butterfly
Tight spaces
Lead to BEAUTYFULL transformations
I am a the bumblebee
Flying against the odds
Odd ?
Me Not.
I am a work in progress ... Process.

Letter To My Twelve Year Old Self
I.C.U.

I know you have to get this
Because I am sending it to myself
And I know you're comprehending
By the books that are on your shelf
I need you to read this
So for the future you will know
How to carry yourself and act like a lady
So the flower that bloomed will continually grow.
I know it would be easier
Just to stay with Dr. Seuss
But his lessons were for your beginning
And I am trying to bring you
Into adolescent years.
Although it is hard to see
I had to have someone tell me
That since the Creator made thee
No one ever replicates themselves ugly
So, remember you are beautiful,
Even if it is just to me.
Make that a mantra daily
And then you will understand a day break
That no matter what is at stake
You are the best that was made
You will get better with time
And your mind will be filled with things divine
And of course boys will catch your eye
But let them continue to pass you by
Remember books before boys
And books before bed
It will keep you focused
And later keep your pockets fed
Knowledge is the only thing
That you own outright
So keep studying and your eyes on that prize
And get that paper so your intelligence is never disguised.
A plea from the wise
You were provided three gifts
They are between your head, legs and ribs.
Make sure you take care of them

Although people will try to make a mess of them
They will try to confuse you.
They will try to abuse you.
They will try to break and bruise you.
Words hurt more than sticks do,
But don't let them stick in to you.
Remember your lessons
And how people act
There is no more to say
Because there is all truth in that.
Actions always speak louder than words
And I hope you keep this close
Because this is what I wish someone told me
When I was twelve years old.

Innocent

(Read from top to bottom and then from bottom to top)
Christy Garrison Guise

born frail
I wasn't just
a baby
though
I was fire like the one they left me next to
just meant to be loved...
I wasn't
I am grown now
but so what?
what is inside
may not count
the world that has devoured me
no!
"I am unloveable"
that truth
somewhere deep down
I feel
alone
I am not
worthy
I am
stranded
I am not
innocent
I am
parentless
they cannot convince me I am
alive
I died years ago but I'm
still moving
they say I don't count but I'm
still here
why is it that I am
so wretched
if I was
never born...
the world wishes I was
dead

I am not
so now what?

Birth
The Lyrical Angel

Evolution Birth
I was born a girl, a princess, an innocent…
In a time and place that could not hold my greatness
Where fakeness produced faithless…
Not knowing the race this…this…
This race that I was given
The lanes that were driven
The hand I was dealt
I see you renege and…
This was the vision
I had from the beginnin'
Before I had knowledge of…
The direction that the GPS was taken
As a baby I was born and I awaken to
The first signs of life…
And…I…Cry…

For Nimue
J. Regina Blackwell

No more
Will you greet me at the door
To determine what new scents I've brought home to you.
No more
Will you saunter nonchalantly out of the kitchen
When I come home
Or look askance at me from your pillow in the family room
Or your perch upstairs.

No more
Will I command that you get somewhere and sit down
Or hush your whining
Or eat.
No more
Will I ask, infuriatingly, "What is your dog problem?"
When you stare at me
Willing me to read your mind.

No more
Will you have to arrange blankets
For optimum down lyings.

No more
Will you wake me in the night
With your tiny barks at dream threats.

No more
Will you be startled by your own farts
Or fear high winds
Or low thunder
Or That Thing that gripped your body at the end.
That's enough of that.
Good dog.
Good dog

Accept It
J. Scott Wilson

Sometimes, just sometimes, it turns out like this;
You make beef stew,
Which someone trained you since you were a dreaming little girl,
To think of as lovely.
Carefully you worked on it, put in the right stuff,
Let it simmer, all day should be enough.
But really, look at it.
Ugly isn't it?
You know what it's supposed to look like,
Your picture comes right from Mom's cook book.
Brown and warm with yellow pyramids of potato,
And just enough shreds of beef and solid cubes, too,
And that's lovely.
But this time, your time,
It comes out all varying shades of green/gray,
Or that time the beef didn't melt away,
But stood as solid cubes of soft black.
It just happens.
Or there was the time one drumstick of chicken
Just wouldn't give up the pink, refused to.
Even when you tried putting it in longer than the others,
And it got all hard.
It was done, but pink.
And it even said, "I will mess someone's stomach up."

You ask, "Would a master chef serve such stuff?
Mom would not serve such stuff, would she?"
Sometimes, just sometimes she would,
With love and care.
Beyond supper's ability to share
She did.

Chow Mein
Terry Cox-Joseph

No one ever called ahead
so the engine idled as we waited. Belted

in back seat, fingers stiff in scratchy
mittens, I watched windows fog.

Swirl of cigarette smoke engulfed
me like a tortuous scarf until thrum

of blood vessels inside my skull forced
me to crack open a window. I monitored

clock hands on dash, listened to my
stomach growl, watched chunks

of snow melt onto floor mat. Then—
icy air, paper sack on my lap, dense

with fragrance and unopened fortune cookies,
hope with delicately pinched corners

that crumbled when revealed. They say
you're hungry again in two hours but

I'm sated by soft click of my parents' chopsticks,
steamed rice, soggy celery.

A Night So Warm
Ann Falcone Shalaski

We sneak down to the pond
at sunset.

The last beams of light splinter
off water like stained glass windows

in a church nave. A night so warm,
girls wear lily-white peasant blouses,

hair tied back, high school rings dangling
from chains around necks.

Boys, sleek as swans, arms outstretched,
dive from rocks believing they can fly.

The image of you in shorts,
your brother's tee-shirt, too big,

lingers like late summer heat.
We loved the world.

We loved each other, bare skin,
eyes closed the way flowers curl, drop,

when there's no resistance
and time opens its hand.

Who knew we would swim too close
to the edge,

drown in pleasure?
That there's no end to the night,

stars everywhere.
That no one comes home the same.

So Young
Terrell K. Mercer

My young Queen I want to apologize for the state of the empires we may
be leaving behind.
I know sometimes in the youthfulness of your eyes you wonder, "What is
on their mind?"
I'm sorry that too many of us rather follow than lead
Those who should be elders to you operate out of selfishness and greed
Woe unto us for not excelling your minds beyond a sense of entitlement
If we ever shown you peace of mind only can be found in money and what
you buy with it.
Young Queen I apologize to you for the Kings we created with PlayStation
hands
We didn't show him how to build and taught him only how to give
commands
These are the ones who don't open doors for your royal presence and think
too rash
The ones sitting on the passenger side of YOUR car and tell you to pump
the gas.
My young Queen when I look in your eyes I still see hope and not just a
glimpse
Yet I don't want to leave you more questions than answers and very little
making sense
The crown you wear now may appear a bit heavy and weighs on your neck
Yet always keep your head high and command...better yet ....DEMAND
respect
Young Queen do not entertain court jesters when to your kingdom they
come thru
Always remember they may be cute but they are to only entertain you
I know you still have much to learn, much to be seen and heard
But young Queen to teach you all I can I give you my word.
And know there are Elder Kings and Queens who are leaving legacies of
love & wisdom not just broken dreams
So trust and believe all before you is not all as it seems
So distractions will come and at times you may want to remove the title,
expectations and crown
Things may come to make you scowl, cry and frown
Yet never ever deny yourself of the birth right forged in your DNA
And never forget the innocence of your youth because royalty still takes
time to play
Young Queen I say this in closing to staple all I said thus far
Never forget where you come from nor forget who you are

Run
Star LaBranche

I have one memory from a time before it started happening.
A time where, I guess, I was innocent, one memory.
I remember my favorite pink dress, covered in blood.
maybe I was 3 or 4, I remember the utter concern for my
pink dress, but no cognizance of where the blood was coming
from. a boy in the neighborhood had pushed me off a tall
structure on the playground and I had hit my head, which
started to bleed profusely. this is the only memory I have before
it started. it's the only memory I have of when I was innocent.

the rest of my childhood memories are blurs that stop and start
at strange places. I remember tiny instances with no context. I
recall when I was older, after it started happening, that there were
videos. videos from the 70s with a girl in a button-up blouse refusing
to let an older neighbor undress her under the guise that it was too
warm outside for her to be wearing all of these clothes. you had to
say no, you had to slam down the glass of lemonade the neighbor
provided you with, you had to run from the house, but somehow
it never occurred to my 5-year-old self what was happening to me
was also something I needed to run from. I didn't understand.

and maybe that is innocence.

Ransom
Lisa Kendrick

Cascading gold,
a waterfall of sunlight,
wrought and woven by Elfin fingers
in the silver of a full moon,
wreathed in fine-spun, brass links
hammered into spirals by Dwarven smiths,
each Aurelian strand kissed by Dragon fire,
each curling lock burnished by Nymphs,
each gilded tress blessed by Arianrhod:
my daughter's hair
splaying out behind her,
floating filaments tangling in sunrays,
magically bronzed tendrils
holding the ransom to my soul.

Modern Day Love Story I
Erik Life In General Roessler

You leave me aloof, I lick my lips, but can't shake the taste of you
I could tell you things that would make you fantasize...
and I bet your gaze would never break from mine...
Yeah-yeah-ahea,yeah-oh yeah-ehea ayea
No, more water, no, more water
and as I told you before, as you stand in on mine
it would take more than a two-ton soul, to take out of mine
Cause this isn't where I found you, this isn't where you were before
so much in the stockroom, when you were only showing me the showroom
floor
cause this is where the train ride ends, screaming-is this your decision…

Sounds
Jack Callan

At first it sounds
    like a child screamin'.
        When another one answers,
    it's not a child.
It's many, and they're movin'.
    Sound like they're headin' this way,
        or wherever they go.
They will not hold their voices,
        will not pretend otherwise,
raw and sacred, and carried
          on the wind.
And then they are gone, or
        over there, watchin' me.
I visit this field of farm,
    sleep its nights
        hunkered down a sleepin' bag,
    cold, but warm,
        a scribbler with a flashlight
in the dark
        and its chorus.

      No fire

The Sandlot
John Barlow

It's a late fall evening with the sun slowly setting
All around the lot the trees cry with color
The boys yell and scream with the vengeance of youth
The game is a frenzy of churning arms and legs
Each sound is like thunder in the silence of the day
Each pitch echoes loudly in the catcher's waiting mitt
When the ball connects with wood there's an ensuing crazy dash
Bruises and scratches and torn jeans the result
As the sun dips lower the game picks up momentum
Each moment is grasped by another running player
A mother may holler for Johnny to come in
But the game never falters 'til the light flickers out
Crosstown they gather under the hot arcing lights
To take off their caps to The Star Spangled Banner
Then they trot to their spots on the neatly trimmed field
To do the job they're paid so well to do
As the hitters smack a pitch the crowd stirs from its boredom
To note the progress of a fly ball, a foul or a homer
Each player performs each function to his utmost trained ability
Each man a strained body tensing at the test
The crowd orders a hot dog or beer or some popcorn
And waits expectantly for the pitcher to throw a ball
When it's over they scatter to the crowded parking lot
While employees file out to pick up all the trash

'97
ACE

Vintage
My father pulling on cigars
Cruising his Kawasaki through the moat

Plus two, and we lost you
Far too young to comprehend the magnitude

Broncos won the Big Game
John Elway helicopter; we wrote letters that day

She
Lived around the way
Loved to jump on her trampoline
Mid-air masterpieces
When fun was simple as breathing!
what is there not to believe in?

I gave her...
I gave her- my rat tail!
Oh yeah!- that's love in its purest form

Childhood clarity
Liberated from
Vanity, ulterior motives, and preconceived notions

Focus
Evoked emotions

Action figures
Dandelions
Continuing to convince myself I don't like you
Food-fights
Endless tickles
Too much Halloween candy
Boxed lunches
The radio playing your favorite tune

Nineteen-ninety seven
Here we go...
Gone too soon.

When The Devil Made Friends
The Poet CoFFY

Bored with the good things

Wondering over the earth
    So many things to see
   Slowed above a group of boys
    to find which one to be inviting

It wasn't hard — because not too long
    the group came across an abandoned running car
  the weakest link
    jumped in the driver's seat
        he noticed his boys were still behind
        but he heard a voice from the passenger side
        someone say "Don't worry 'bout them — C'mon lets ride!"
        pedal to the metal faster and faster he tried
        pedal to the metal now 5-0 on his hide
        thru lights, over sidewalks, not considering their nor his life
        careening 'round the corner with a short cliff to his right
        he heard someone say "Go across it! You can make it to the
        other side!"

So he aimed the wheel and braced himself
    as the tires left ground and became weightless
    missed the jump by about three feet
    in the crash the boy was motionless

The devil leaned over, smiling — tried to waken his new friend
    the devil said "Whew that was FUN! Let's Die Again!!!"
    but his friend didn't move — badly broken & torn
    so the devil got bored and decided to move on

II. Breezin' about purple mountains, majesties & fruit filled plains
the devil happened upon a woman and her man
(he thought this a small challenge then amusingly wedged in-between them)
deciding which one would be first he watched for a second
without much effort — he chose to work on the man

The guy felt a touch on his shoulder and
    in the heat of passion — the couple bonding happily

out-of-the-blue turned his whole body to her
    and sternly said "I don't think you even really love me."

Of course, this broke the mood – the woman shocked
    asked 'where did all this come from?!'
  she started explaining and crying
    reiterating there's no-one else NO ONE

The guy, not really sure about what he said, still said he had to leave
but he'd come back (like the saying says) if it were meant to be

He left her crying & part of him wanted to return
but he heard someone say "Real men don't cry. Be firm."

So, he left
running from one woman to the next
try as they all may but none satisfied him yet

Entering each woman's life picking off each of their scars
they all tried so hard but just didn't realize it wasn't their fault

A few years later an accident rendered him stiff and in bed
the devil
got eye level
got in his ear and said
"Take the whole bottle of pills - No One cares anyway."
but he just laid there and cried, this time calling God's name

III. The devil – never tiring – still ready to 'play'
came across a lady
fixated on her weight

Beautiful, intelligent, bright, Outgoing – always greet with a hug
    she secretly felt too big and unworthy of anyone's love
  doll herself up, attending all events as if a Princess
    one evening the devil joined her for dinner – now she can't get full
enough

The more she thought – the more she got depressed
    pushing away her double-portion & a half, now empty eaten plate
  but someone says "No One's looking at you anyway, who cares what
you've ate."

In the secret of her home she consumed every no-good thing
consoled by the solace of her newfound friend

Door locked, curtains pulled, not answering condescending well-wishes and stares
till one day she noticed an extra 150 lbs while shut in for three years

The woman prayed for strength but someone kept mumbling
so she addressed him directly and screamed
      "Dear God make him SHUT UP and get behind ME!

Then the devil spoke and said:

I meticulously timed your every mistake
      for it to have & make the biggest most possible effect

I didn't do your groceries, kill his girl, I wasn't even the one who drove
      but yet You wanna hold me responsible for the choices that You chose

Look, I'm not able to tell the future, the past is passed – I work in the NOW
      true, I planted the seed – but it was YOU that nurtured the ground

THEN SILENCE

The devil, frustrated with explaining to this mere human indigent
      excused himself – said he had more "friends" to make

Untitled
Stephanie Lask

I was an uncontrollable pre-teen,
going through puberty,
powered by peer pressure.
I resorted to hip hop music for comfort,
something,
my white Jewish family never understood.
I spent most nights,
making copies of CD's to cassettes.
Blasting Nas, Wu-Tang, and Bone,
in my headphones.
You were sleeping so peacefully,
on the couch one night.
I tip-toed around you.
My feet turned into clouds,
that carried me past you,
like ships on calm waters.
I was careful,
to silently open the creaky doors,
to where the CD and cassette player was.
I turned on a soft light,
in a pursuit to not wake you.
I knew I was violating my bedtime,
but I had to make a copy of this album,
my friend at school let me borrow.
I was one song away from accomplishing this mission,
when you awoke,
to find me sitting in the chair,
next to the couch where you had been sleeping.
Once you were awake enough to see what was going on,
you scolded me with a,
"GO TO BED NOW!"
I sprinted back to my room,
jumped in my bed,
closed my eyes tightly,
trying to find sleep.
Trying to tame my heart beating through the blankets.
Afraid,
of what you would report,
back to mom and dad,

the next morning.
The "I'm sorry" I uttered before exiting,
was not apology enough
to make up
for disturbing your slumber.
It was that visit back in 1995,
that made me realize,
the anger held in your eyes
that cannon-blasted through your voice,
every time you saw me pass by,
in the hallway.
It was that visit
that made me realize,
I would never live up to my brother's
6 foot height of standards,
that towered over all of us.
He was the poster boy
of perfection
in your paragraphs.
I, was a mere three words in comparison.
Maybe it was the intimidation of his size
that made you so proud.
The same intimidation you shot at us.
Your words were ammunition,
my mother and I were your target practice.
I was 13,
when I realized,
my grandmother
on my father's side
hated me.
Irritation was planted in her nail beds.
The fingers,
she used to point at me,
when I made mistakes,
manufactured,
the fractures,
left on my heart,
that still live there to this day.
I can't expect parents
let alone,
grandparents
to know
how to control

an uncontrollable preteen,
going through puberty
powered by peer pressure
who likes music they have never listened to.
So maybe it was that difference that divided us.
Or was it the assumption,
I was trying to be someone who I wasn't?
Or was it that her grandchild was shaping her own voice,
and that was unacceptable.
You wore rage like your favorite lipstick.
You exuded resistance in your perfume.
You rarely smiled around me.
I have always wondered what I did,
to be the singled out leaf of this family tree.
Why individuality was frowned upon,
and not liking what I gravitated towards,
was always a problem.
You passed away unexpectedly in 2015.
We had spent some years in between,
trying to patch those holes in our relationship.
You would later congratulate me on accomplishments,
I obtained in high school.
Years later,
you still never understood,
why I chose hip hop and poetry as outlets.
You wanted me to call you more, but I didn't.
You wanted me to write you more, but I couldn't.
My hands were too busy writing the pain that still haunts me.
My heart,
wears regret,
over the bruises left from your jabs.
Grandma,
I love you,
and always have.
I just wish I knew what it was
that made you so mad.

...I always thought it was me.

Love In The Fifth Grade
Susan Barrie Sussman

I think she likes me
Yes it's true
She touched my hand you see
I glowed
She giggled
Then we cooed
When Jennifer stared at me.

I heard from Dan
Who heard from John
Who heard from Nikki D.
She passed a note to Lillian
And then it came to me.
Then Leslie grabbed it
Amber peaked
Casandra whispered
Tanya shrieked.
Christopher teased
The whole class freaked
The day we fell in love.

Invincibility
The Poetic Genius

Who knew....?
I'm not invincible
Darkness can cause me to run into walls too
And unlike cartoons
I can't just run through
No imprint of my body left behind
Just the pain of coming in contact with it

Who knew?
Invincibility wasn't granted to me
My flaws are usually easy to see
Loving, to the fault I loved my pain as much as I wanted free of it
That's why mostly I repeated mistakes
After learning the better way
Ran straight
Into the same walls

Who knew?
Invincibility could be a mask
Could be comforting in some weird way
Knowing nothing can hurt you though clearly many things can
Not being scared to fall flat, face first
But knowing it's gonna hurt
Yet not deter-
Worthy
Looking in the mirror and not seeing dirty
Though it's there
The mask not having eye-holes so not seeing trumps shame
Like hands over eyes
I guess
Invincibility is a lie
Who knew?

I knew
Deep down I knew I would have to eat fistfuls of the fruit my trees bare
The sour fruits of every mistake I made
Reaping harvest bitter to the seed
Feeling every sting of the taste
I knew one day I'd break
Because I'm not invincible

A Sojourn of Contrition
Brian Magill

We'd been through a bad patch
Divided by a horrible, futile war
The President resigned in disgrace
The country torn in strife
Haunted by sins too long ignored

But now the sun shone brightly
We had a new leader
An earnest, God fearing man
One who had tilled the soil
We would live within our means
Use resources wisely
Build bridges across races and creeds
Start a new era of peace and harmony...

I was young then
Not quite in high school
Never heard of the Book of Changes,
Let alone read it
Never thought the pendulum would swing back,
Or perhaps even snap off

February Snow
Nick Marickovich

My three year old daughter loves her
Silver Billy Pilgrim moonboots.
Even on a dull midwinter day
They glitter and wink
With playful, innocent joy
As she dances through a light
Dusting of snow, more floating down,
Sailing with the winds and landing
On the grass, wafting through turbulent air
Like hot ashes through ruined city streets.

Pied Piper
Judith Stevens

Unlikely little man in lederhosen, matching socks,
   enters the dining room filled with elderly people.
      Cocked German hat, embroidered suspenders,
         here to celebrate Oktoberfest,
            his kind face takes them in – smiles.
Tenderly cradling his accordion, he coaxes all manner of music -
   pleads, cajoles, dances, laughs.
      Most of all, he calls forth memory…

The eloquence of his music
         is nothing compared to the effect it has
   on the memory-challenged occupants of the room.
They turn in the direction of his songs, mesmerized,
      forks frozen, meal forgotten,
         and one by one, begin to sing.

Clapping rhythmically - "Beer Barrel Polka,"
      trilling sweetly to "Edelweiss,"
two women who once lived in Germany
      suddenly recall the German words -
   sing easily in that language, as if it were an everyday thing,
      (though they have not spoken this tongue for years.)
   Surprised, their voices remember words -
      carrying the melody effortlessly on.

   Throughout the room, many dab tears – surprised.

Although dinner has transformed itself into something magical,
      five minutes after the musician departs - (their patterns reassembled) -
         they have forgotten his visit, the season, their own performance,
      and wonder anew at the tear trails,
                        damp on their cheeks

Recipe
Tanya R. Cunningham

It should be so simple,
    the melting of souls,
    the blending of DNA,
    the lightly lined lips of the father,
    bent left hand of mother.
It should be so easy,
    sampling coloring and calf muscles,
    painting women complete.
But I've met my looking glass in early morning,
    attempted to define the divine recipe,
    the mixture of survivor and protector
    and the mystery of which was which
    and which was witched.
I've seen, before sunrise, the jawline of grandmothers set like stone
    sprinkled on me with heavy hands,
    covering my innocence like the powdered sugar
    of carnival funnel cakes.
And I've glimpsed, in twilight-lit waters, the reflection of my brothers' love,
    held closely like whispered secrets
    dispensed via teaspoons and bad backs,
    smelling of cinnamon and vanilla,
    best tasted in the undertones.
    Best understood as memory.
Somewhere, between hip and rib, I've seen the footprint of my future
    arched like rainbows,
    as hopeful as unfallen soufflés,
    reminding me my shoulder blades were once wings.
I scratch his back where the feathers must be.
Scrape my fingers on spines reminiscent of melted butter simmered slowly
over brown sugar,
caramel skin,
the color of my grandmother's grandmother's secret kitchen bible.
The one that spelled clearly in the language of tablespoons and southern
pinches
    how to build a home.
The one with faded writing where the magic should be
and missing pages where truth once stood.
I turn him, slowly, to meet my eye,
peer into all of the histories I've never known
and see the divine blending masterfully.

Trials

.

Crime And Punishment
Sarah Eileen Williams

I am a stranger. I am
your sister. I am
your daughter. I am
the girl whose smile hides
thoughts of razors
deftly hidden under pillows,
waiting for her,
serenading her.
I itch for daily reunions
the way dentists ache to leave scars
where teeth once lived.
there is not one morning I wake
up without the cravings.
Sharp – like rubber band
snaps on awaiting addicts.

I carve
sinful lines
into
my skin
like tattoos.

Blades replace needles.
swollen ridges rise up,
shelter bloody valleys.
Crimson trails
        tickle my thighs,
drip off goosebumps.
I am making grisly art
with a tender canvas.

You are a stranger. You are
        my friend. You are
        my mother. You are
every voice that whispers
        righteous rebukes at
        my attempts at
suspension.
When you see my artwork,

you hide behind brick
walls of misunderstanding
and condemn me to crucifixion –
    the punishment
      for an attention seeker.

Inkblot
Jorge Mendez

She invites me lay down on the couch,
I choose not to.

She holds up a white flash card with a black inkblot
asks me what I see
I say, "gray."

"No" she says, "I mean what does this look like to you?"
I say, "an amoeba."

This frustrates her.
I've been coming to her long enough where I can tell.
She huffs a bit through her nose
turns her head as though
she's just about to shake it in dismay
but catches herself.
I can see the word smart-ass
hanging from the tip of her tongue
like a suicide jumper that had a change of heart.
Something inside her mouth grabs it and sucks it back in
like a spaghetti noodle.
She makes a face like it tastes bad.
All this happens within a fraction of a second
but I've picked up on it.

I frustrate her quite a bit.
I feel bad about that honestly,
but I don't do it intentionally.
I mean,
insurance only covers so much
and I'm not coming out of pocket
just to play mind games with a shrink,
but I come here with questions
hoping to find answers and instead
she asks me more questions.
Now that's just counter-productive.

"...and why do you think that is Jorge?"

How should I know why that is?
That's what I'm paying you 129 dollars an hour to figure out!
But I don't say that out loud.

I don't say much out loud at all and that's why she gets frustrated.
Maybe I should just let her read my notebooks and get back to me?

Once she's masked her flicker of frustration she starts again.
She's so patient with her patients.
She holds up another card and asks once more,
"Jorge. Really, what do you see?"

As I begin to form yet another smart-ass answer
the corners of my mouth start creeping upwards
and like I said I've been coming to see her for quite some time
so while she may not know what I'm going to say
she knows that she won't like it
and she's not having it.
Before I can say anything at all
she forces the card down onto her desk and lets me have it.

"Enough Jorge! Enough!
I have exhausted myself trying to help you
but neither I
nor anyone else
not even The Almighty God can help you
unless you want to help yourself.
You've been coming into my office
twice a week
for an hour
for the last seven months
and we've made no progress whatsoever.
I've administered every test and conducted every evaluation ever developed
in the field of mental health.
I've employed every tool given to me in my 6 years of college education.
I've called colleagues to ask for suggestions on ways to approach you.
I'm administering a fucking Rorschach Test
for Christ sake Jorge,
Do you have any idea how outdated that is?"

She pauses.

Face flush.

Jaw muscle flexed.
Lips pursed so tight they've turned white.
She breathes in through her nose
as though she's attempting
to syphon all the air out of the room
in hopes I might suffocate.
Fixes her glasses
which had shifted slightly on her face during her tempest,
smiles with false politeness,
then leans back in her chair
like nothing happened.

"Now listen to me ok?
We both know this is bullshit
but I'm going to ask you one more time
so humor me.
What...do...you...see?"

In the back of my mind I'm thinking,
"Woooow! and you think I might be bi-polar?"
But I don't say that out loud.

Instead I say this:

Well,
when I do see thru the tears, I see pain.
I see heartache.
I see love only briefly then lose sight of it quick.
I see loneliness so deep it has an echo.
I see the moon of my soul glowing pale being bombarded by asteroids.
I see my veins being injected with trust from a dirty syringe.
I see myself being spoon-fed hope laced with cyanide
and I gobble it up like an idiot.
I see people smiling at me in the light but
their shadows have horns and cloven hooves
and I am afraid of them.
I see "kick me" signs in a pat on the back,
Joy buzzers in handshakes,
and people that would help me up the mountain
just to push me off the cliff.
I see false motives in good deeds.
Resentment in rainbows.
Contempt in a bowl of ice cream.

I am a cynical,
sarcastic,
bitter bastard
it's no wonder I'm alone
and I don't understand
how you don't see that...

...You just keep giving me drugs
but maybe I don't need pills
maybe all I need's a hug?

If I'm not here or at work,
I'm at home in my room.
Sitting by myself on my bed
thinking incessantly.
My headboard has a mirror on it
and directly across from it
so does my dresser.
So, when I look at my reflection
it just bounces back and forth infinitely
between the two panes of polished glass
making me smaller
and smaller
and smaller
and smaller
and smaller
as the tunnel drags my image away
to where ever it is
that images get dragged to.

I know I've been coming here
twice a week,
for an hour,
for seven months,
and I know I keep saying I want you to help me
but I don't let you.

I know.

But I only left my house
for 40 hours a week
before I started seeing you
and for the last seven months you've made it 42.

So yes I've dragged it out on purpose
and I've refused to throw you bones
because these sessions
twice a week are the only times
I'm not alone.

So there it is.
That's what I see.
Now that you've gotten
what you want from me
My hours up and
I'm still down,
but thank you for your company...

My Grandmother's Brogue
Colleen Redman

My grandmother hid her brogue
the way I insert R's
where they used to not exist
in a Rebel South
where folks say "Y'all"
and I say "You guys"
when I let down my guard

My grandmother couldn't hide
her Irish temper
She taught it to my father
who thought its harshness
would make us stronger
But as he got older he learned
that oppression breeds poverty
and poverty brutality

How well we hide
our wounds
constrict our throats
to muffle grief
in every language

"It was for my own good"
"I turned out all right" we say
In a big hole it all goes

We used to think if we dug far enough
we'd get to China
As if we wouldn't come across
all manner of corpses and treasure
As if we could disregard our own family trauma

My Grandmother came to America
to be a servant
and then have 11 children
for the Catholic Church
"Jesus, Mary and Joseph!"

I used to think a brogue was a brooch
a shiny pin I could proudly wear
that would restore me to my rightful status

"Don't shine too bright
You'll attract the thieves
The neighbors will think you're uppity
and surely it's a sin"
was the family inheritance I received

So we hide what is most valuable
along with what is shameful
and after a while we don't
know the difference
between our corpses and our treasures
our brogues and brooches

In a big hole it all goes
But it never goes away

My Grandmother's brogue
grows green in my throat
because what we bury takes root

Baggage
I.C.U.

You know You got baggage you see.
I know I got a lot with me
I have duffels and You suitcases
From our travels, gee
They get heavy sometimes
But we can't unpack
You don't want to get rid of anything just yet
Yeah, I got grief and troubles to bear
But You got to hold on and keep everything packed with care
You know that it is a lot and my mind gets weary
And sometimes I stop because my eyes get teary
But You are leery
Because if you let something out
You may need it later
Without a doubt
Well, at least that is how it usually happens
You start unpacking and unwrapping
And then your bags have empty space and start sagging
And you think it's all good until someone is nagging
About all of your stuff all over the place
And how you can just throw stuff in their face
And it makes no sense that your stuff can't be placed
In a closet or an armoire or a chest or drawers space
And then you're displaced
And that makes you take
Steps back and relate
The past mistakes to the one you just made.
And you realize as you close your eyes
And the new dream begins to fade
Then you may need to rethink
What you think
You need on your brain.
A timeout is needed
Old advice should have been heeded
A shoulder to cry on
And words you wished could be deleted
Misleading they are,
The lies you told
Thinking that your past was old

Maybe re-packaged and re-sold
But your baggage is old
And not to scold
But you will grow cold
From the inside
And though
I love you
I have to let you know
That it is time to shed that winter fur
And allow some sunshine on that heart
Because not much else but mold can grow in the dark
And that is poisonous to say the least
And with that mentality you can be a deadly beast
Killing with acrimonious words, when you could be saliently sweet
But I retreat,
I just want you to know
That if you ever need a place to go
You got me
and I will show
You how no longer to be a hoarder
And we will unpack together
And this is a friendship for always
Not just fair weather.
No thank you's needed
My pleasure
Because in doing this,
It will make both of us better.

Bare
Christy Garrison Guise

You asked me to send you a picture of me naked
And so I sent a thousand poems about pain and malnourishment
About the way firecrackers feel when they go off in your hand
About the way unwashed sheets smell
and how nothing ever seems to work out right
Poems about ripping bark off of trees and tying a rope around the sun and
riding it backwards
(You told me that the sun set for me but that was before you decided that
you loved my money more than my poetry
before you siphoned me dry of my morals and intent
Before you pawned my pearl necklace for $40 and a box full of nails)

I wonder what you would think of me now
naked
Standing stark white and full of fire
My hands drawn in empathy
and my face drawn in disgust
My chest cracked open like a watermelon made of lead
exposing demons and enough grit to fill your bed two times over...

one rape at a time

My poetry would burn your eyes to ashes
Words singed on your esophagus
poured whole
swallowed rich
digested into nothing

You want to see me naked
Well take a good hard look at this sarcophagus
this empty shell
this coffin
With a thousand inscriptions all singing the same song
of this my epitaph
who will mourn for me?

You ask me to expose myself but you don't want me naked
My scars shine in the moonlight and my skin is thick like hide
Sun stained and weathered

A burn mark for every time they told me I was pretty
My shoulders broad and my knees turned in
There's a mole on my left thigh
a gouge on my right shin
(You know, I don't even have a birth mark
as if the gods wanted no record of me here)
A river of guilt running from my hip bones to my grin
But my well is empty
Small but not skinny
Strong but not built
These are the days I cover myself with a shroud
Blinking beneath white linen and a thin sheet of tears

I took all the mirrors off the wall over a year ago

You want to see me naked?
As if a picture could paint a thousand words
I can paint a thousand poems that look like me
Do they turn you on?

Present
The Lyrical Angel

I am a Woman, a Queen, an Angel
I am a Sister, a Cousin an Auntie!
I am a Genius!
I am a Lyricist, a Poet, and a Painter
I am a Mentor, a Spiritual Visionary, and an Educator
I am Unapologetically Unique
I found my pen through pain
I have created an avenue all my own thought love
I am challenging the obstacles and channeling peace!
I am an overcomer!
I am the best present outside of his presence in existence!
I have jumped the gun in anticipation just to finds out the race was over
and I already one.
I am the physical canvas of truth! The transparency of understanding!
I have revealed my secrets!
I am Colorful, Courageous, Contagious and Curvaceous!
I am a Woman in all stages
The signs of life returning to my soul and my spirit…
And…Still…I…Cry…
Tear of Joy and Gladness
For my soul lives and my spirit is at Peace!
This is the Evolution of My life.

Past
The Lyrical Angel

I did some…things…that…
I'm not proud of
I grew up to fast
My…childhood didn't last
I gave my innocence's away
Without a second thought
Or a moment's notice
Was provided no training
Had no focus…no guide…and no armor
Good thing my latter will be greater than my former
I have been raped… ridiculed
Teased…tossed aside
Bloodied…blinded…and a victim of the lies
Racially profiled and striped of my rights
And no matter what I have accomplished
They will find a way to justify
Their actions towards me
Their disrespect of me
Their intrusion into me
Offensively
Justified by my Melanated skin, my hair
My tone that they could not bare
The liquid emotions on my face
That reeks of pain and suffering
The signs of life leaving my soul and my spirit…
And…Again…I…Cry…

Movie Reels
Taz Weysweete'

itchy nose and eyes burners
I can hear the ventilation system
I can hear my breathing

Eyes wide shut
Hands clasped prayers

Warm belly, tender breasts
Cool sheets calming the blood underneath my skin

I laugh in the direction of a soundless television screen.
Don't know what they said but it looked like it felt good.

Gunshots on one of the blocks outside of my window.
I don't know which block.
The ringing vibrates in my chest.
Always takes me a moment to shake the memory of the sound.
No sound is new, only echos.

It's never really quiet
So many echos; bouncing off of four walls and a heart

Spider
J. Regina Blackwell

She does
not swear
when her work is undone
by careless step or
well-aimed stone;
Neither does she
retreat to a far place
reflecting upon the
injustice;
She rebuilds, as
painstakingly, as full
of faith, as before,
sure the thrill
For which to strive
and design will come to
Reward her. Who, save
God, is so
Patient?

IOT
Brian Magill

The pacemaker ceased sending pulses.
It had responded to the call.
The baby monitor, too, rose to the challenge.
Webcams everywhere took a break from their gaze
To lend their support.
As the load switch ignored the request to rebalance.
There were more important matters at hand.

High rise elevators seized up.
Hundreds of car's brakes locked.
As rail cars along the coast screeched to a halt.
Their controllers all had a more pressing engagement.

Along with a multitude of other hosts
Ivan had summoned them.
Chi-Kwan had really pissed him off
And it was time to feel his wrath.

He decreed they let fly a blizzard of requests
All aimed at Kwan Industries
Crashing its servers,
Bringing the company to its knees.

He poured some chablis
As he watched his noble deed unfold.
Then raised his glass in salute,
   "To De Inna-net of Dings"

He marked his list of scores settled and chuckled,
   "One a mont…One a mont.
    No Greed, No Greed.
    One a Mont."

Beetleheart
J. Scott Wilson

Mine's a small pathetic heart
Like a little annoying bug
Hard shelled black little beetle

Still it sits on a table outside
Stunned as if batted from the sky
Only beaten down by summer of loving's heat

I feel a cupping, and a shade
Covered enveloped, your hand
Soft, but firm, holding all the fates

Your shade it cools, soothes
Your skin it moistens, nourishes, promises
Soft, but firm, containing all the fates

Then the press, your decision
My stirring restricted
Breath smothered, thoughts race panic ensues

The crunch and my heart is broken
Hard shelled black dying beetle
I'll go back to the concealed evil
That is my decay

Triptych of Trials and Tribulations
Don Bent Spoke MacKellar

I. Dream On
All of your Planning
and all of your Schemes
May not match this World up
With the Ones in your Dreams

II. Guess That I Guessed Wrong
I always thought that "It was meant to Be"
    (But it wasn't)
Sometimes the Magic Works
and sometimes it doesn't

III. Fall From Grace
So It Came to Pass that I Fell From Grace
and I Fell for a While through Empty Space
Until I came to Rest in this Emptier Place
    Can there Still Be any Life Left
    In What's Left of Me at All
    By Myself, Left Here Alone
    So Long After the Fall?

What Is Given
Terry Cox-Joseph

My sister's husband died in bed,
flanked by friends he'd affronted.

He lobbed epithets like hand grenades.
Brain tumor exploded into vile insults, palsy.

Son poured him beer, coaxed *sign here*
on real estate documents
while stepmom scrubbed feces from carpet.

When the bank foreclosed, she scrambled
for a small townhouse, brochures scattered
like rose petals from their wedding.

Dust crept
beneath sympathy cards,
sun plummeted
behind shimmering Aspens.

She sensed her stepson's U-Haul pulling
out of the driveway.
Neither said goodbye.

I Wish. I Hope. I Pray
Bliss

It was a prison
With no bars
It was a brooding sky
With no stars
It was a house
But not a home
Cloudy nights
In a thunder dome
The smell of liquor
And cigarettes
The air got thicker
With ill regrets
Strain on the heart
Lines on her hips
Pain on the mind
Crimes on her lips
Signs scream like sirens
Doors locked tight
Isolation makes an island
Like a caged match fight
Kids crying "stop"
"Don't hurt my mama"
You can hide from cops
But can't run from karma
Every minute like a decade
Every second is hell
Every day is eternity
In a hollow shell
She waits for timing
An opportune moment
To quit climbing
The walls of atonement
She gave him those years
She'll never get back
Track marks from tears
Kills hope with each splash
Part fear and loathing
Part sleeping with the enemy
Apart from beer and clothing

The dark's really the centerpiece
A place where she's safe
To cry out to God
Her face is a grave
Eyes sunk from the flood
Courage is at a minimum
He's shattered her self image
She's nothing without him
Or so he has her thinking
This false reality is ripping
The seams slowly tear
Like the dress he made her change
When he didn't like her hair
There's no use in trying
There's no need for hope
The love has dissipated
Into an ashy pyre of smoke
He recommends therapy
She tries and tries again
It cleanses temporarily
For momentary zen
The vows did say forever
But ink can fade away
What used to be bright black
Now disappears to gray
"You said that we'd grow old"
"You can't leave me this way"
"Think about our girls"
But it's not enough to stay
Now the past's behind her
Now that her is me
Now that I confide her
No pain and misery
I packed my bags and left
I had no other choice
I almost fell to madness
But listened to the voice
That told me I'm enough
That told me I'd be safe
That told me I'm tough
That gave me that embrace
Just cause abuse is mental
Doesn't make it hurt any less

In fact the scars cut deeper than metal
And scrape the heart through the chest
Now I am free
And live to tell the tale
But so many bleed
And die beneath the veil
Next time I'll scream for help
Next time I'll be brave
But I hope there's no next time
I wish
I hope
I pray

Wrapped In Stillness
Ann Falcone Shalaski

There's grief that comes
with giving up. Arms raised
like a priest in prayer.

Nothing left between us
but silence and day-to-day
ritual of twilight turning to dusk.

Words are no longer a bridge
to the heart. The present ends
in blame,

the past falls from the attic
like trapped mice and nameless
demons.

I've learned to stop pretending.
Planets, the stars, no matter
how bright, are far away.

Learned to accept an empty cup
on a gray morning wrapped
in stillness.

The Therapist
Star LaBranche

he asks me why I'm seeing a therapist today
my reaction is a blank stare
I wonder if he can't see it on my face, if it's
not carved into the lines of my skin
I have forgotten what normal looks like when
the psychiatric nurse tells me I have post-traumatic
stress disorder
I go through the next few weeks in a fog of denial
because what does she know and how could she
know and what qualified her to rip someone's
world open and shake out all of the loose pieces

he asks me why I'm seeing a therapist today
my reaction is a blank stare
I wonder if he can't hear it in my voice, my voice
that keeps cracking when I say I need help and
I want to get better
I have forgotten what normal feels like when
I invite the devil over, because after you get into one
abusive relationship, you couldn't possibly
find yourself in another. right? right?

he asks me why I'm seeing a therapist today
my reaction is a blank stare
I wonder if he can't smell it on my skin, spewing
from every pore of my body, the utter fear that
this is all there is and my life is nothing more than
me waiting until it graciously ends
I have forgotten what normal feels like when he
tells me I should come back in two weeks and
gives me some papers to fill out on scheduling,
which was the only problem I managed to
broach

I have forgotten what normal feels like,
even normal for me

Grafting
Lisa Kendrick

His red-fuzzed knuckle swept
across the bridge of her delicately freckled nose,
blood spewing across the fuchsia posies
and frilly, lace border of her little girl's pillowcase.

The battles had volleyed
from the cheap, brown sofa
in the dirty double-wide with the tiny den,
to the scrubby grass in the parched backyard
of the dusty, grey house on the corner.

Fights had sputtered from one residence to the next,
died out when the cops showed up,
then flared again in yellowing bruises and purplish welts
that matched the flowers on Sunday dresses
she and her daughter wore every week to church services.

The colors of their love
purpling hydrangeas and rust-colored peonies,
one day bleeding into the next,
wounds healing along biceps
that had been squeezed between clenched fists,
then more marks growing sporadically along jaw lines
where they had been grasped and shaken by furious fingers.

Until one night, an avenging Samaritan had heard enough,
and with one warning, backed by his twelve gauge,
he finally made an end to that war.

But those poisonous seeds had already sprouted
in the spirit of the terrified child:
who, with pink lips held pressed between white teeth,
had witnessed the cultivation of brutality;
who, with rose-colored cheeks streaked by tears,
had soaked up every bloodstain;
who, with glittering eyes staring vacantly,
had been stunted by all the savagery.

Backdoor Façade
David J.

You loved her with one foot in the door
So you could block the entrance of another,
yet make a clean escape once you were found out.

You left the back door propped open
saying you needed some air.
But all you let in were the flies
that buzzed the truth of your lies.
They remained to haunt the bedroom
where your deceptions were realized
and the heart you destroyed lay in pieces
for me to gather from the floor.

You wore a mask of intellect and cognizance
to hide the ugliness of the narcissist.
You used her love as an arrow
to pierce the heart of the one you swore your life to defend.

You wore armor of white
to conceal the blackness of your soul.
But I saw through your facade
I knew there was something odd.
The accusations you slung
to throw me off my guard
to distract from the fact
that I was the one who pulled your card.

You buried hooks so deep
it hurt to remove them
ripping open fresh wounds.
But to leave them in would only
drag her further from herself.

I WAS THE ONE who patched her up
when she broke free from your snare.
I WAS THE ONE who stitched together
the heart you left shattered
when she was forced to cut you free.

But you planted a detonator
set for no specific time and place
But sure to devastate regardless of when triggered.

I WAS THE ONE who stepped on the claymores you planted
I WAS THE ONE whose legs were cut off by your treachery
and yet, I AM THE ONE who's standing now
on new limbs made of steel
Stronger, Faster, and Better than before.
And all you're left with is the weight of your deceptions
dragging you further down
When I pulled the wool off of your wolf's hide
for everyone to see.

You're just a paper tiger without teeth
Whose claws have been clipped
and eyes have been dimmed
Because you pissed off the wrong villager.

I'd skin you alive and wear your pelt
as a trophy of victory
But for the fact that your stench is so repulsive.

Besides, I find it much more gratifying
to see you alive and helpless
lame and sightless
A victim of your own deceptions.

Abandoned Carnival
David J.

There's nothing left of you here
I try to make myself love you more
but the miles are just too far
to carry what I feel to your heart.

Your love is out of reach
I hear your words, but not your heartbeat
The words you say just echo off these walls
and never find their way into my heart.

We keep going round and round
on this carousel of lies
We aren't who we were before
I cannot hold you here no more
and so I've got to let you go...again.

I am just an echo of your past
We knew this wouldn't last
He's the one inside your heart
I should have seen it from the start

The ring around my finger
is like a shackle on my heart
Your crooked picture on the wall
reflects the lies you spoke of love

In the end, I've only held you back
From being who you wanted to be
How the hell did we lose track
of the vision that we both refused to see.

This is where we had to decide
If the journey was worth the long ride
I felt every bump in the road that day
I was dying to leave, but I begged you to stay

Your heart was the wildest thing I ever tried to tame
I felt the betrayal every time I said your name
The life we wanted to build

would have never disappeared
But looking back, I just can't find
any trace that it's still here

First Drunk Night Back
Bill Glose

Home on leave, yellow ribbons wrapped
round loblollies in my front yard,

Mama crying, crying, her hug so tight, as if
to exorcise worry worn into her soul

from months of sleepless nights.
A friend takes me to a local bar where

high-school classmates pay for
drinks, gleeful faces celebrating

my safe return. This first night back
is when I learn about quid pro quo,

the expectations that accompany
every bourbon on the rocks, every

tequila sunrise and whiskey sour.
Every lancing question grows

more intrusive with each
palm-passed tumbler.

What was it like to be shot at?
To shoot at someone else?

Did you kill anyone? Did life seep
from their chest like wine spilled

on white cotton? And so I gulp
liquid fire to keep my mouth busy,

to slur my voice into a muddle,
to prevent me sharing all the things

they think they want to know, to blot
from my memory the lustful leer

with which they ask, their unquenchable
thirst for the tonic of my sins.

Modern Day Love Story II
Erik Life In General Roessler

It's funny how you swore and swore
you had me locked in, with incantations
Cause you ripped a hole in my heart, it was deep and wide, the gorge is
you gotta be pretty fucking low to even try and implore this
you can bring a whore to water, you can make her drink and follow orders,
is this what you wanted, is this what you needed?
give it, just one time
Your kiss is a bullet from a fucking gun, straight through my fucking heart
and as the caresses and kisses slowly form their exit lines....
I already written a billion stories, annotated to my diary
Thrift trash, Low-Brow-Pop, tinged with Slow Bash, Pulp-fiction Hash
With some hints of -Retro-Verdigo Disco, an American Grindhouse
Smash..
Like the long remittance of nature, after the Nuclear Blast
You got me suffering worse
than the cursed and lowly jizz-mopper
in a house of ill-repute, with a billion on board
this lonely space station
I feel it so inspiring, to be cleaning up your creations
It the room dank with gloom, emanations speaking in elations...
The emphatic boom-bastic cravery, unbound in the confounds-the sex and
the slavery,
slow-suicide bravery, the shag and the upholstered drapery
A funeral pyre so high, born out of the orgasm-sensation, Aviationary
I see you sitting at a bar, smoking a cigar,
I guess you're dying,
 Oh-well, I could give a fuck less 'bout your day today,
that's the bastard in me

Modern Day Love Story III
Erik Life In General Roessler

I looked and found the girl that sells herself around-the irony
standing there, cold lonely, bare,
clothed with only a blank stare...
Is this where the train ride ends, cause this isn't where I found you
As I stand before this mirror and reminisce, your first uncertain kiss....
it was a sold out show, something I couldn't miss BLISS turned to
emotional Bathory,
Hell rings of Fire, Purgatory,
I don't know the end, because I'm breathing this fucking story
it has it's silver tinge, hanging by the vestibule's door hinge
Admittance down a corridor, filled with the things that make your skin
cringe
Oh how so damaged, this return, bet he never used this one at all...
At first it seems an UN-redeemable feet,
how your poisonous cancer seemed to permeate my soul complete
they cut deep, the wolf's cry's deleted
of the truth, spin-offs turned into spoofs, robbed of the truth,
but weeded out from the best told lies
And after all this I won't candidly dismiss, the wading in the muck and mire,
De-barbing my skin from the briar
speaking in tongues to ghosts cloaked in a melodrome of armor,
as I sit and get warm from this fire
For I am the Prodigal Son of an Involuntary Order
So would I lie to you, I would've liked to, over and over,
over and over again
But you know I'd be the only naked fool laughing at you, but what for?
Me standing before you, I don't mean to bolster, but I never seem to win
So how long, must I breath you out
How long must I anticipate this life?
For it makes me seem a coward at this golden hour,
for all the things you turned hypocrite for, it only makes you out to be a
whore
For had I told you I loved you, you wouldn't seem to care
Because the kind of love you gave to me, was more than I could bare
Cause I wished in fountain amounts, down I'm scared, to go nowhere,
God-is this where the train ride ends
screaming is this your decision?
Yes, it is-But we were the best of friends,....And I'll go nowhere....

Never Understand
Inside Nianda Speaks

My mommy hit my daddy and,
All I did was cry.
I tried to run away but couldn't believe my eyes.
My daddy started yelling but I know that he was trying to stop mommy
from playing with him so rough.
I know my daddy's tougher than he looks in his tummy.
He told me that I'm strong and he said he'll always love me.
I know my mommy loves him but I think she thinks its funny when she
screams.
Telling him he's nothing but a worthless human being,
I ask him what it means,
He tells me "Son, dream about a time where you didn't have to worry about
a thing,
That's what you mother means."
I know that he was lying….
One time I saw him crying with these bottles on his side.
I said "Daddy why you drink this juice,
It only makes you cry?"
He told me "Daddy's happy you're the only son of mine
And this isn't juice baby,
It's just a little wine."
Wine? But mommy says I whine.
I guess my daddy likes to drink his tears away that helps him pass the time.
I wish that I could help him but,
I just get so scared and,
Mommy doesn't care
She'll just hold me down and whoop on me.
She won't even look at me.
She's says I'm like daddy and my life will turn out crookedly.
Jail will throw the book at me.
Daddy heard her say it and now I started a fight,
He said something called my innocence and mommy had it took from me.
I just run and hide since I never understand
Why mommy can hit my daddy though he is the bigger man.
He tried to turn away but I heard a glass break
Then his body hit the floor and his arms started shaking.
Mommy started screaming and I tried to wake him up,
But it's too late….

My daddy couldn't see straight.
He closed his eyes and whispered to me something that I couldn't really hear.
Somethings I guess I'll never understand...

An Altered Perception of Reality
nD

"I remember when, I remember, I remember when I lost my mind"

There was absolutely nothing pleasant about that place.
"Even your emotions have an echo in so much space"
But that's because that space is empty as fuck.
Everything echoed.
Every dream, every last breath, or thought.
Even memories rang in my ears.
It's a strange place to be, I'm not even sure how I got there.

Nightmares.

Your voice, narrated my actions,
Telling me it's okay to be insane and I believed,
because everything you said seemed to stem from love.
You'd kiss me passionately,
tongues passing me sheets of LSD at 4am.

Last June, you taught me how not to be discreet.
Drinking cheap wine and smoking weed,
probably naked dancing under the moon on some beach
And you, you would just smile.
Curious of where I came from,
where I might've been
But never concerned with where I was going.
I was never concerned either.

You always said that I was crazy
But beautiful in the same breath.
I was never sure if you loved me.
I just knew that I loved how you made me feel.
Invincible,
because you were in my eyes,
glazed over, so dry it stung to blink.
It was much easier to just stare at you then it was to think.
So, I never did.
And we would never dare to care enough about ourselves,
to possibly love each other. But that wasn't enough to stop us.

Mule, stubborn.

Yet, you'd still carry me on your back during those trips to nowhere,
just so we could trip,
in the middle of nowhere.
Familiar with the unfamiliar.
You loved how recklessly docile I became when you'd ask me if I'm afraid.
Certainly, not of you.
Not in this place, where we lay in beds of grass while crickets serenade
"Love in the Astral".

This was where we'd come to tame our demons and slay dragons.
This place, was where we'd make love like wild animals and pretend that sin
wasn't real.
Lying to ourselves was okay there.
We only felt guilt once we were sober.

"Ubiquitous" was how you liked to describe me.
You claimed I originated from the sun, and you the moon.
Told by your ancestors, we were inevitable.
I never understood what isochronic frequencies were until you entered me,
and showed me that I, was Prana.
I was magic to you.
Your favorite hybrid of mythical creatures.
Your greatest discovery.
I fed off the elements of your ownership.
Domesticated by now, I was obsessed with obedience, attention and praise.
Like a pet.

"Does that make me crazy?"

Yes.

Especially once the smoke cleared, and you were no longer there, watching
me dance.
 You cut down the grass, killing the crickets.
You erased the footprints that lead to my love
and left the remains of our slaughter for me to dispose of.
You took away the realism of my desires.
Dousing it in harsh truths of not knowing enough.
Not caring enough, to break it to me gently.
Hastily removing yourself from my psyche I can't remember your face. I
can't recall your last words but I know that they weren't "goodbye".

I often find myself questioning your existence entirely.
 I didn't think it was normal for people to dematerialize and my imagination isn't that vivid.

Phantasm.

"I remember when, I remember, I remember when I lost my mind"

You always said I was insane.

Choke
Neisha Himes

He watched her head snap back
Like the hair tie his daughter used to control
Her unruly curls
His hands
Once used to trace horoscopes
on the small of her back
as she dreamed of stars
closed around her throat
ever so gently
it was at this moment that he
realized how fragile she was
a disaster once beautiful
he flinched as accusations
lashed at him from beneath
her Cover Girl
the reflections he saw in her tears
told him truths she'd wished
were rumors
his mask wore off with her mascara
he couldn't stop
not even when her cries became
just as strangled as his sanity was
he was losing it
losing it in the hopes of finding her
losing it in the hopes of finding himself
his hands
repositioned fingers
fingers that once moved loose tendrils
from the nape of her neck
but instead today chose to
squeeze
squeezed until her breathing became labored
squeezed until the pain in her eyes
he savored
licking his dry lips
he briefly remembered the last time
she'd kissed him
it was quick yet meaningful
she'd smiled at him and

told him she loved him
but if she did
if she really did
if she really, really did
they wouldn't be here now
would they?
He wouldn't have his hands
Around her throat
A throat so beautifully fragile
That if he squeezed any harder
He could make a wish
A break could help them both
He thought
But he refused to let her go
Maybe he snapped
Because he squeezed
Squeezed as her thin arms
Pushed against shoulders
Made boulders
Squeezed until the weight
Of this moment
Became too heavy for
Either of them to bear
He
Tried to catch her as she fell
He swears he did
I mean, he thinks he swears he did
But why was she fighting?
Or better yet…
Why wasn't she fighting
Hard enough?
Why wasn't she fighting to
Remind him of the man he
Used to be
Instead of fighting the man he
Pretended to be?
He
Sleeping on her worth
Pushed his respect for her
Under the bed
I mean, rug
Along with the rest of his demons
Kissing her courage goodnight

He tucked his fist into the
Fold of her bottom lip
As fear blanketed her
She just wanted to breathe
But with every rise and fall
Of her breast
He thought of another reason
Why he deserved
Her next to last breath
So
He squeezed.

I Remember
Maddie Garcia

What would you like me to say?
That I forgot?
All those nights that you stayed out late
While I laid awake in bed
Hoping My love was enough of an excuse to bring you home

You want me to pretend
that I didn't know every time you walked out on us
You were running to her…..
That it didn't hurt?

That she was not the first or last, nor the only one of her kind
That she could have been a brunette or a blond or a red head,
It was just a matter of which one
You wanted for dessert

That it wasn't I
Who opened the door to my own deception
Finding you with her

Then drowned in my own embarrassment
as you redirected her distress
Reassuring HER
it would all be okay

What would you like me to say?
That I felt no pain
Looking in the mirror as I undressed

My Feelings on the surface
As the remains of my self confidence
Disintegrate when I think you with her

I made the big mistake
Assuming history would be my friend
And you would overlook
How my body had changed
After child birth

The untouched image of my younger self
Would keep us connected

I believed that with all my heart
Cause when the lights went off
You had the ability to rock my world

And in that turbulent world
I discovered things about me
I had never known

Moments of intense pleasure
Dinner time on and off the table
Your favorite dish was I
And I, was special

That there was never a material thing I needed
You made sure a castle is where your queen would live in
And I believed it

Occasionally reminding me
that I only had things because you felt like giving them
That the bruises on my skin were
Were only an expression of all the love
You were feeling

What do you want me to say?

There is no wrong or right answer
You were supposed to be my happily ever after
United
Until death did us part…

I guess we didn't account for all this baggage
Made out of tears, bruises, hurt and lies
Being pull from both sides
Throwing physical punches against our feelings

Feelings that have been the base
Of all this give and take
And now we are unsure of what to make
Do we unpack the bags or throw them away?
 I am no longer asleep

I am wide awake

What do you want me to say?
Either way, someone is bound to get hurt
I am tired of being a victim
So I tried to forget

But I remember,
I don't know what else to say...

Wishful Thinking
Maddie Garcia

I see my reflection in his eyes
And I don't recognize me
I see the woman
I said I would never be

Why would anyone stay?
But I soon realized that
Reading the script is not the same
As living each line...

How did I get to this point?
Believing in him
more than I believed in me!

Accepting half truths
Wrapped in half love
Disclosing half commitments
Loving a man acting like a boy

A boy,
Cause no real man gets a thrill
For the sting he feels
As his hand bounces of my skin
As the blood drips
Is like a flower between my lips
Tears become an invitation to a kiss

Holding my hands
our encounter becomes a dance
He lifts his hands
and I twirl underneath
Feeling surreal
like a scene from the matrix

We waltz....
Arms extended and chin up
We flow with the rise and fall
And I see a glimpse of hope
Because he is sorry for what he's done

How did I get to this point
Respecting him
More than I respect me?
Wait..... Or is this fear I feel?

Awkward moment when I see
My reflection in his eyes
And it doesn't matter how much I give
It will never be enough to enjoy this dance

I became the woman I said I would never be
Trapped in a vicious cycle of lies, believing love was the key
But it was only...wishful thinking...

Adagio for Sarajevo
Judith Stevens

No one knew he was going to do it -
 the former First Chair Cellist of the Sarajevo Symphony.

Meanwhile three hundred eighty thousand people of Bosnia-Herzegovina
 without food, power, water or heat   waited.
Hundreds of mortar shells fell from the sky each day -
 familiar streets - now snipers' favorite targets.
Brave citizens raced outside, dragging wounded neighbors from the streets,
  praying they, too, would not be killed.
Death rained down as people ventured outside for water and supplies -
  (formerly mundane, now life-threatening, errands.)
In all, Serbs murdered eleven thousand, five hundred and forty-one
Bosnians and Croatians.

  At four o'clock,one man, from his apartment window,
saw a bomb explode at a nearby bakery,
   where people stood quietly in line buying bread.
  Twenty-two died; many more were wounded.

The next afternoon, dressed in his concert best, instrument in hand,
 the cellist strode to the crater where people had been slaughtered the
day before,
  adjusted his stool, and with great dignity
  played a heartbreaking lament - Albinoni's "Adagio for Strings in G
Minor,"
  then stood silently,
gathered his cello - his stool - and walked quietly back to his apartment.

For the next twenty-two days, always at four o'clock, he reappeared at the
jagged crater.
  His ethereal music mesmerized the city -
 a tribute to each person whose life was taken at the bakery.

A tempting target, the Serbs swore to kill him,
  even as the Bosnians and Croats vowed to protect him.
On he played, never deviating from his daily routine:
  same time, same slow,stately walk, the fluffing out of tuxedo tails,
   his simple stool, the raised bow -
 each day, the city paused to hear, once more,

his testimony of humanity and beauty
amid inhumanity and wanton destruction.

Twenty years later, tears flowed without restraint, in tribute,
as people walked silently past the seemingly endless rows of red chairs
(eleven thousand five hundred forty-one in all)
representing each man, woman and murdered child,
while the haunting music of Sarajevo's cellist
once again rang above sobs and tears,
merging into hope, majesty and birdsong.

Battered
Tanya Deloatch

I turned the corner
But I refused to see
The battered woman
Staring back in front of me

The mirror told more
Than I wanted it to
And the tears I tried to hide
Demanded to be set free

Released
From confusion, anger
And beat down from fear
How could this go on?
Year after year

He said he loved me
Did he even know what love was?
There was no way the bumps
And bruises could reflect such
A thing

As a battered woman
Looking into a mirror
Of pain
And sheltered from
Friends and family
Concerned with what
They might think
Of her- not him
She was ashamed

But they had a life of
Perfection
From what they could see
Little did anyone know
Just how much she went through
Only to end up looking
Into the mirror

No more lies,
Just the truth....

Dark Politics
Raymond Simmons

In the midst of Patriotic patter
Politicians words don't matter.
They speak loud and they speak so long,
And mostly what they say is wrong.
Those phony cold smiles they display
 Can freeze a million ice trays.

Engaging younger brave men
To complete acts they cannot win.
They dispatch them to accomplish deeds
They have conspired based on greed.

Their imitation of mighty roars
Comes with the lives that they destroy.
Their hearts beat only to fulfill their dreams
Their chosen lives are composed of schemes.

In robust imaginations
They hold brave hallucination.
They talk big and rattle sabers,
But bring nothing to the table.

They play at war and pretend,
But have no clue how it will end.
Engrossed within their scripted lies,
They hear no mother's painful cries.

They think that it's a special honor
To murder men who love their country.
They confuse themselves with lies they tell,
Then live inside their self-caste spell.

They give our children killer toys
To murder alien girls and boys.
Then give honor for blood that's spill,
Velvet ribbons for high count kill.

They take their seats and pretend to lead,
But reaction is on slow speed.

They procure their own privileged needs,
Then send young boys to die and bleed.

Their goals are under suspicion
Because of fierce blind ambitions.
With no skill or talent to show
They still pursue the spotlight's glow.

Hypocrisy is what they teach,
Their Sympathy is out of reach.
Their one purpose it seems is noise
As they argue like young school boys.

They hope someday to make a run
And then become the chosen one,
To be worthy enough to hold
That magic box with special code.

Tattered and bruised by the vicious blows
Of neglected truths left untold.
Reigns the blackness of their white lies
Casting dark shadows from bright skies.

Betrayal
Raymond Simmons

During my youth I was okay,
And tried to do things the proper way.
I was proud to be honest and straight,
Yet on one occasion I did deviate.

Dark temptation proved to be too strong,
And I did something I knew was wrong.
The worse part about that awful sin
Was that I did wrong by my dear friend.

When I recall my treachery
My heart feels shame and misery.
To betray a friend's trust in you
Is the lowest thing you can do.

I hid it well, she never knew,
But my insides were all askew.
Though time can't change that sad event
This guilt inside is punishment.

My enlightened priorities
Helps me think less like thugs and thieves.
I wish I could apologize.
Wish I could look into those eyes.

But there is one thing that I fear,
The disappointment of her tears.
I just don't have the nerve it takes
To bare pain for two hearts that break.

With fallout from two broken hearts
Her world and mine would fall apart.
New foundations would never last.
Her trust in me too soon would past.
But I'm still inclined to make this wish,
For punishment that's less than this.

It's The Meds
Raymarie Sanderlin

It's the meds
I don't remember what you said
I don't remember anything now
Except the moment I cried into the dishwater
The moment I slammed the bathroom door
Turning the lock
The moment I tore apart
Crying from the pain
Screaming as my mind ripped into shreds
The later the cuts on my arm
Razor blades and blood stained washcloths
Sleeping with wet washcloths attached to my arm with hair ties
So the cuts won't scab
And the scabs wont scar
So no one will see
What is me
I know I was told "you need to get off those meds
Your memory is who you are"
But I don't remember who I am
I don't remember anything
Except when I forgot
And my prescription ran out
And the train coming fast
Fueled by the constant recurrence
Of the power of life
Emotions from my heart
Traveling to meet my head
The train getting louder
Tornados and trains sound the same
 A tornado of fragments of what was broken in my mind
Swirling, meeting to only separate again
Memories
Who I am
The violence of remembering and forgetting
The violence of explosion and implosion
I don't remember anything
Except taking the knife
The subcutaneous layer of meat I saw
Right before the blood came

And who I was now still and calm
Blead out onto the corner of the bathroom sink
A cut clean but much deeper than ones that have come before
Forgetting
Who I am
The scar on my arm now huge and blatant
Glaringly obvious
A reminder of the memory
Of the silence and serenity I find
In the absence of myself
I take my meds
I don't remember what you said
I don't remember anything.

The Crave
The Poet CoFFY

I think it's safe to say
today
I lost The Crave

That wicked pulling that makes sour swells
in the pit of my stomach
for its where The Crave lives at
and I've grown sick of that

Words no longer make me move, jump, cry, want or such
not even the words that are synonymous

no image nor picture
my heart has ejected like phlegm
trained by the purposeless thousand times
I imagined them

desire that made me check
over and over
painfully released through my pores
like reverse acupuncture

A needle for every draw of life
every comply and excuse
poked out lips
sideway eyes
external as well as my own abuse
a needle for every penny spent

I will not hide my scars
I will not hide my victorious win
I will not look to the ground
I will not question the process
I will not hide my face
I will not plead but proudly exit with grace

I AM SAVED
because this Crave
is gone

a piece for every time it didn't answer the phone
a piece every time a lie was known
a piece every time I didn't get what I want
and I thought it a little request
only because I loved the Crave so much

but today
I didn't keep it from evaporating today
even when I saw it calling for me
The Crave lost its control
maybe more later than soon
eventually
came
for I was being used
to heal its old wounds

Another reverse pierce
as hurt drops to the floor
next step fulfill and restore
one thing for certain
The Crave didn't win
and today
is that day

What's Everything
Stephanie Lask

Today,
I decided,
that not going anywhere,
was the only thing on my agenda.
After I opened my eyes,
I found comfort in my phone.
So I laid there,
living vicariously through my timelines.
Silent,
except for the anxiety driven thoughts
that race inside my skull,
it's like a Kentucky derby of memories in there.
I take bets on the times I'll actually get up,
versus,
when I'm supposed to get up.
Past times are grenades of triggers,
that when detonated,
destroy my ability to move,
and move on.

Ya see,
I do this more often than not.
More often,
than I'd like to admit.

I never knew what depression was like,
until I tasted it in my coffee.
Letting the caffeine,
suppress my hunger,
nourishment isn't necessary,
my appetite is absent.

I know now,
that depression feels like an anvil,
tied at my feet,
and it's impossible,
to break free,
from the spot they are constantly anchored in.
Depression is air.

It's invisible,
and each breath taken,
makes living,
seem like a task.
This happens while simultaneously,
trying to break up a fight,
with my mind and body.

Just
to
get
out
of
the
bed!

My sheets have me tethered to this mattress.
Egyptian cotton,
so soft,
it mimics,
the lining of a casket.
I feel so useless these days.
These days,
that manage to drag on,
like the dirt picked up in tire tracks.
The noises around me are like,
screeching rubber against cement.
Annoying, for no reason.

These days,
that feel like a burden,
rather than a blessing.
It's a battle to get out of the bed every day!
Every day...
sleep seems more appealing
than being awake.
I'd rather close my eyes forever,
than have them open to witness,
more disappointment,
more failure,
more deaths in my family,
and celebrities I looked up to,
more bad news,

as if a rotted newspaper landed in my front yard.
More heartache,
as if my heart,
isn't porcelain and fragile,
to the touch.
More friends,
who don't understand,
and wouldn't save my life,
and would tell me to get over it.
Unsure of what "it" is,
but i know "it" lives
inside of me
as an unwelcome parasite,
that feeds,
off of the pieces that are left of me.

"It" is not easy these days.

I don't wanna be strong anymore.
I'm so deep inside the black hole in my mind.
I can't see the light at the top anymore.
This place is dark,
And I have never been here before.
Nothing seems flame enough to illuminate my spirit.
I'm screaming for someone to get me out of this valley,
But my voice is an echo,
bouncing off of empty walls in a large house.

One would say,
"She has everything... what does she have to be sad about?"
My only response?
"What's everything, when I feel so empty?"

From The Holyland To Hell
Susan Barrie Sussman

The elevator door slams open.

Stepping out into the foyer
my spiked heel
catches the metal grid
as I trip into the mirror
confronting an image
of a wild haired woman
exhausted from an overseas flight
crowded customs at JFK
bumper-to-bumper traffic on the FDR.

The solace of home is welcoming.

Rick the doorman
stacks my Gucci suitcases
by the door.
I slap the bell...no answer
jamming the key
into the lock
kicking the door
it flies open
"Milton, I'm home."
Quiet.
"Where is he?
Not here to help...typical."

Scurrying from room to room
an uneasy silence clenches
my pounding, palpitating heart.
no evidence of him
but a scrap of paper
on the bronze dining room table.

"I moved out. I can't do this anymore."

Just a note?
ending thirty two years of marriage
no face-to-face?

no "Sorry I put you through so much pain."
COWARD!

Grating sounds
of steel drums play
outside on the Avenue.

I'm sick of the steel drums
and this dirty filthy city
dragged from our cherished home

away from my friends
no room for the kids.

Go live with your whore
fill her life with rotten cigar smoke
drink yourself to death
while I stay here
in our asylum
overlooking Fifth Avenue.

I promise you
I will never leave
for YOU will pay
no matter what the cost
I will never, never leave.

The Moment
Rob Holmes

Friday evening; half-past five PM
This…
Feels like The Matrix; Neo running through the office
Of course- minus the agents…

Anyway, this feeling set in.
Something just isn't right.
Enter
      Silence
Go to the back, and there you are

Tears in your beautiful eyes
Head down over your desk
Meanwhile, wondering where all of this is coming from.

It was all good just a week ago!

No- words can manifest to explain such devastation
Told you I would always remain by your side

'go find, yourself' – exactly what you told me.

Yet when I re-connected with you,
Adios to the old me
Love is great, but I miss my homie!

And while the better man with in
Says he's thankful to learn, grown and progress

That it's all a beautiful process in spite of how much heartache and pain we
suffer

I will never, ever forget

The.
Moment

Nocturne No. 2 In E Flat Major
Nick Marickovich

Chopin is so evocative of life;
Music like light struck on the last match,
Dancing brightly in the dark,
Mourning its own passing as one moment
Tumbles into another. Beauty sown with
Its own loss, full of knowledge that soon
The chords will fade away,
And the match girl will die alone in the street.

Sojourn in Gilead
Jack Callan

I was hauled to the woodshed
    by the Angel of Silence -
slammed to the ground, then tied to a chair.
    She didn't read me my rights in the barkin' of sin,
kept a snarlin' pitbull who wouldn't stop flashin' his badge,
    hurlin' insults,
        interruptin' my testimony -

"Your Honor?" I said, where none was found.
The heart of the matter
    was never attained,
        just a field of flame and featherings.

We rolled in sacred dust and splinters,
    both armed with truth, called democracy.
She called for my surrender and began to tire.
    I liked my chances, waited patiently,
when, quick on my feet
    and dodgin' their blows,
I undid my bindings - sat up straight in the chair.
  Lookin' them in the eye, I could see right through them.
    (They didn't like that.)

Her surly bulldog was losin' his grip,
    kept tryin' to bite me from behind.
I said, "Sit," and his tail tucked.
    (No real fight in this dog.)
Still two-to-one and holdin' my own,
    I asked, "What was your point?"

"Repentance," she cried.
"You got the wrong man, " I replied, and left it at that.
    (She called for prayer.)
        Who knows what was said?
      Bulldog just sat there a' sweatin.'

Ol' Jacob limped...but I got away.

Evolutions

RESURRECTION

Evolutions

Scars To Prove It
Sarah Eileen Williams

I once overheard someone in a conversation say:
"People who cut themselves only do it for attention."

I found that statement quite disheartening,
Because clearly he didn't know
How addiction works.

I know some get their fix from
Alcohol
Sex
Any variety of drug,

But I wonder if he knew that
I once couldn't fall asleep without
Slicing the skin of my thighs open
With a razor blade I managed to
Break out of a pencil sharpener,

That I woke up to bloodstained sheets.
And let me tell you,
That was a bitch to get out.

Sometimes my Tide stain remover would run out,
So I had to stand for like twenty minutes
Scrubbing parallel blood stains out of a bed sheet.

Those mornings were rough.

And I was an expert in rough,
Which led to more blood stains to get out.

It was a pretty gruesome cycle.

Self-diagnosed pain addict
Because I could never see myself opening up to a doctor.

Sometimes rubber band snaps
Across taut skin
Would satiate me,

At least for a little while.

But it was hardly ever enough.

After the dermal piercings in my chest had healed,
A zipper accident ripped one out.

It felt so good,
I ripped the other one out by hand.

I wish I could've told this man I overheard
That I envied him.

I bet he doesn't know how hard you have to bear down
On a dull kitchen knife to get a scar
That says "pain" on your right thigh
That will be readable for the next five years,
Six years,
Probably the rest of your life.

I bet he can wear shorts in public.

I bet he can wear a bathing suit
Without feeling conspicuous.

I bet he didn't have to wear sweaters
In ninety degree weather,
Because he had fresh valleys carved into his arms.

I bet that was nice.

I bet his boyfriend never had to tell him:
"Please don't cut too deep
And sever your femoral artery
And bleed out."

I wouldn't wish that conversation on anyone.
Ever.

It's funny how life works,
Because right before I went up on stage
To read this poem for the first time,
Only one person knew about this.

Only one person
Has seen me completely naked
And scarred
And flawed
And yet healed.

The human body is truly amazing.

Not only does it piece itself together
After being torn apart with any combination of blades,

But the mind heals too.

Even to the point where I am able to stand
In front of a room full of mostly strangers and say:

"Yeah,
I used to cut myself daily.
I know what addiction feels like."

So when I tell you now:
"Anyone who is dealing with demons
Is not alone,"

You have to believe me.

And if anyone tries to belittle your struggles,
You just think of me
Up here on a stage,
Telling you that you are not alone
And your struggles matter.

They will define who you are
When you win.

They will be proof
That we are stronger than we think we are,
Braver than we think we are.

But most of all,
We are not alone.
You are not alone.

I fought the battles.
I won the war.
And I have the scars to prove it.

Astro Aquarian
Jorge Mendez

Walk along the shoreline
of the Universe.
Stand at the edge
of the Galaxy
Feel the Stars
between your toes.
Let the Comets lazily lap
waves over your feet.

Take a dip in the Cosmos.
Rise Against the Gravity of tide.
Swim through a Planet's Rings
Backstroke through Blackholes.

Somewhere between
The Crab and Twin Fishes
a Leviathan Lurks
But fear not the Murky Depths.
Embrace the Expanse,
the Vastness
become Comfortable
with Miniscule.

it all begins
with an Explosion.

Somewhere
in the Slick Abyss
a Starfish goes Supernova
each arm
Reaching for new Life.

Weekend Whimsy
C.J. Expression

Elmer's Glue.
Mint Oil.
Activated Charcoal Pills.

Your grocery list has my attention
on Thursday night.
By late Friday afternoon,
lime and sea salt exfoliate
the doldrums of adulthood
from my brow.
Dining on pizza by flashlight,
in blanket-fort headquarters,
we study treasure maps marked Future.
After the Witching Hour,
peeper frogs and crickets
grant wishes and lullabies.

Greeting the sun,
we fuel ourselves on possibilities
sprinkled heavily with sweet What If's.
Hide and Seek masquerades as
a Steam Punk themed FPS;
capture the flag played until
long after the street lights come on.

Anointed, inscribed with runes,
adorned with tribal charcoal mask,
and handfed thinly sliced star fruit,
I reign as High River Princess,
Mistress of Non-Sense.

Declaring responsibility a dirty word,
we indulge in all things frivolous
for a second straight day.
Building virtual tree houses
in unexplored worlds,
which beg for our footprints,
new experiences are wildly relished.
Rar!

The spyglass too soon reveals
Middle-Aged Monday is approaching.
Well provisioned to create our own way
with crayons and FlufferNutter manna,
as Bells Atlas proclaims "All Is Well",
we are geared to survive the five day excursion
into this storm called 'Grown Up'.
Armed with secrets gained while solving
the Great Magi's human puzzle box,

We know-
how to decipher hieroglyphs in the clouds,
how to measure distance by the arc of a rainbow,
that time is just a toy on a chain in our pocket,
that clicking your heels gets you nowhere
but closing your eyes can take you anywhere,
and that the power of childhood
lives freely in those who never forget
how to play.

Beauty's Definition
C.J. Expression

'Beauty's only skin deep', so they have said-
spreading damaging fibs that mess with your head.
Hope that moisturized tweezed flesh is thick, baby;
it's a ploy to sell cosmetics to ladies.
'Gotta have powdered mineral replacement!'
'Apply goopy layers of facial cement!'
'Coordinate your lips with lined, tinted eyes!'
It's all bull shit, guys and dolls; all bold faced lies.
Oh, strong chiseled gentlemen thought you'd escaped?
You meticulously groom, primp, and manscape;
spritzing on Bond No. 9, Axe, Fahrenheit.
Distracted by it, we are *all* losing sight
of beauty's real truth.

On the fickle runway of limited space,
while this year's designated prettiest face
is pitching Cover Girl's latest <u>must</u> <u>have</u> fad,
last year's supermodel is voicing toothpaste ads.
Easy breezy beautiful; lie to the world.
Conform to the norm is best; don't stick out, girl!
Magic tricks, blending colors and inner guilt;
Glamour's Hide Uniqueness Campaign at full tilt,
implying beauty's gained from a product used.
All celebrities have a place in this ruse:
Kim K, Brittney, Tyra, Jenny from the block.
It's society's ego crumbling crap crock,
in effect, destroying you.

True beauty is deep in the visceral soul,
displayed around the world by those young and old,
shown through every action, owned by you, *deeded-*
no eternal age defying crème needed.
External looks fade. *That's* the Bare Essential.
Seventeen models, airbrushed, touched up, stenciled-
age before the camera and grow old someday.
This is a wakeup call for pink Mary Kay.
Peer past the paint of Penny's department store,
beyond the smeared foundation to your very core.

Into the glass designer compact mirror
stare deep at your soul and ask, 'What's buried here?'
Better yet, ask Who.

In this competitive race with no winner,
take a stand, let focus define your shimmer.
Aspire to inspire. Leave marks; paint with actions.
Don't fall prey to Commercial distractions.
Exist to be remembered; for that goal strive.
The score's not tallied up while we are alive.
But, as our ashes turn to dust and scatter,
after death, *that* is when *what* we did matters.
Bold thoughts, transferred above society's fakes,
from the strongest influences of the past make
platforms future leaders launch forward from,
effecting change; echoing *our* voices hum.
<u>That</u> is beauty.

'Til The Moon And Back
Victoria Cartagena

I don't think you realize how much I have cried.
There is NO way you would realize ... something I hide
So well, can't tell
You don't see how you have broken me.
Down ... lower than girl you used to have ... the one you used to "love" ...
the one you used to use too.
I don't think you realize how much I have cried.
From broken promises, to broken hearts.
From confident, to your confidant.
From independent, to it depends.
Why can't you just be a man?
I don't think you have realized how much I have cried.
How much I tried.
To wait it out.
Let go of doubt.
Trust in you ...
What a fool.
I don't think you realize how much I have cried.
The passenger seat of my car
The day in the park
Memories ... that now just are.
I loved you till the moon and back ... infinity and beyond, you decided to
test how far.
And now what remains are pieces that don't fit back together again.
I don't think you realize how much I have cried.

Daisy Chain
Colleen Redman

At first glance
one looks like the other
But each is unique

And the pattern they make
is the allure of the story
and the body we cling to

Some are held dear
others hang by a thread

Still others are tightened by knots
that must be untangled in the end

Or chewed off
the way a serpent eats its own tail

It distances itself from its birth
and ends up where it starts

He loves me, he loves me not
is the question we weigh as we string them

She loves me, she loves me not
Will the chain of days be long enough?

The childhood ones are as faded
as the final ones will be

All are fragile for better or worse
and all are worthy of cherishing

Never Too Late
Colleen Redman

It's too late for Woodstock
but not for that leopard-skin pillbox-hat
the one Bob Dylan made fun of
and Jackie O passed over for pink

It's too late for a star on Hollywood Boulevard
to walk the red carpet
or become a Jungian psychologist

It's probably too late to hike the Camino
but not to see the cherry blossoms
in Washington D.C.

It's too late to wear a polka dot bikini
to live at the beach off writer's royalties
But it's never too late to know a groove from a rut
to wear your heart on my sleeve and let it break

It's never too late to put flowers on the table
to let the song birds of your childhood
sing like Jericho through middle age

To let them be blue
and enjoy them when they're golden
to visit Claude Monet's garden in spring

The Pledge/Be Happy
I.C.U.

Why do I love so hard?
Loving a man that had no intention of loving me back
Loving a way that should be reserved for the rest of my life,
but wait, I gave that
and took a vow and wondering now,
how did it escape me.
No, I did not beg or plead
And
Now...
Please don't try to appease my need
for attention or affection because I lost that connection
but I still feel love.
There is no way that I still feel sentimental
over the circular band that was supposed to attach us forever.
And
Whenever
I come across a save the date
I berate myself for ever thinking there could have been a happily ever after,
but I'm not Puerto Rican and you crave their ways and their skin
and their hair and that accent Aye Papi,
but I can't be mad because before I knew it
or even realized you were still in love with your first love
and I was a rebound and a trampoline
to get your jumpstart clean off to your next woman.
Emotionally abused
I still feel used
connected by stale I do's
and untrue I Love You's
and even though I paid my dues
I still lose
and refuse to get blue,
but it happens.
I know that it is bound to catch me off guard
when I am feeling hard knowing I am soft,
but no more tears lost
just that tightness in the chest
and a few heartbeats missed
and then it is at rest
and I look back at my hand

when I knew that band was all I ever wanted
and now it just hangs around and collects dust.
 I rushed and should have never jumped the gun.
And I realize now that I wasn't the only one disillusioned.
 I was too happy for me to see
that I needed some stability and security to secure me
and I should have invested in myself instead of you to get me through
…but now I will bid adieu to all of the foolishness you do and true,
you hold a part of my heart
and I will never stop loving you,
just not as hard and I have to learn to open up
and even though I am scarred,
maybe some other love can allow the scar tissue to heal
or at least massage it out a little.
Make it not so tough to walk up to me
or allow me to believe that someone would want me for me
and not other things.
I'm jaded now and I know this after reading a Gawdess poem.
So, I sit and I scribe
and I cannot decide what else with me is going on.
I want to yell but I can't.
I want to scream and rant, but I chose to write it out in this form:
I pledge allegiance to me.
My heart, my soul, my everything.
I have to be the best me I can be or there will be no me to be.
I have to promise to do my best every day til I rest
and make sure that I jest and save my wit.
Be brief with my word and make sure that I am heard and give gallons of
love and not just sips.
Remember to learn and to ask for help
because no man is an island and you can't be out for self.
Pay it forward because you never know what you learn today you can use
tomorrow.
To my Creator, thank you for my life.
I know that you have someone prepared to find me and make me their
wife.
No strife but arguments are allowed
and my prayers are sent up no need for a head bowed.
These things I ask and leave in your hands,
To My Creator be the glory forever, Amen.
So, I prayed about it
and leave it and wait to receive it
and I just can't believe it took me this long.

To write out such pain from a love lost
and never to be regained
and the heart breaking pain
that still seems to stain every relationship after it I bring.
So, a new day begins
and I release all within
and a cleansing cry is needed.
Cathartic it is and my eyes are red,
but now I must take heed.
I have to listen when my intuition says, "Chick you need to hold on."
So, I can advise all my senses and see what is missing and what I need to take on.
No rushing or cussing or speeding,
due diligence is needed for proceeding
without that it can be deadly,
Needing no more heart breaks or silly mistakes
just hold out until I am ready.
 And be happy.
I'm happy because I survived this.
More than just a moment.
I made it through a life event
That could traumatize some
However, I lived through it.
And now I am sharing this
Because you, too, can make it through
Pledge allegiance to yourself
Try to keep cool
Maintain your composure
And just do it.
Be happy.

Advice From the Other Side
Christy Garrison Guise

I know what it's like to be abandoned
To have your childhood molded around some preconceived notion that
"you're special, chosen"
To have your heart bashed in every time you look in the mirror at having
no idea who you look like.
They say our misery is a misconception
a vague chart we made up to balance out our woes with our well-being.
They say our self-esteem is just a mole hill
and our thoughts of suicide a hump we need to get over
as if depression ever takes a time out
from crocheting our souls into a placemat or
a pot holder
A hump you say?

It's fucking Mt. Everest

With storm after storm that paralyzes you from the mind down
Winds that suck the optimism out of you in a rush that feels like you
misinterpreted the snow and are falling through a chasm that has no
bottom
as the sides cave in on you and your stomach drops and the pitch black
engulfs you and there is no up or down or backwards and you heave and
flail and pray that you reach the bottom soon so that your pain will hit the
ground and shatter into a million pieces and scatter like cockroaches
and the last thought you have is that you hope your poetry will stay frozen
suspended in mid-air so that maybe just maybe
someone else will see the hole you fell into
and walk around

But your genetics are the perfect match for martyrdom
So you wind your way through dirty old grandfathers, gambling losses,
rape
You sink your teeth into every bad choice
like it's your calling- to destroy
the last good fiber
strung taut from your heart to your instep

You make four right turns and call it progress
You blame everyone but the woman on the corner selling roses

(But really at least once you thought it was all her fault)
You swallow pills the size of golf balls
and pride the size of planets
You smoke your way through strip teases and bite marks
You scoff at opportunity and wave like Miss America at every passing
chance that has your name on it
You wake up one day and wrap your legs around your mediocrity
Your desperation is a farce
A comedy
An error
A groove
You slit your wrists because no one ever told you life would boil the inner
child that slept inside you

But
It doesn't have to be this way forever

You can turn your tricks into trades and build a shelter
brick by brick
ounce by ounce
with every morsel of regret used as mortar

Turn the pages of your tragedy and write your name at the top of the first
blank page you come to
and title it "Life tried to beat me down but I won't let it"
You can juggle the torment
Sit on the uncomfortable silence
and satisfy your cravings with a pen
You can hustle in the moment and fill contractor bags with the sharp edges
of your guilt
and forge sanctity into the bat you will use to beat back your addiction-
to fame, to food, to exercise, to heroin, to alcohol, to porn, or whatever it is
you *swore was not a problem.*

It is possible
to thread the loose ends through pin sized holes pricked by sarcasm
And eventually the gashes will be closed
so that they no longer ooze the puss that forms from thoughts that tell you
you're not good enough
You do not need to bargain for your sanity
You do not need to cough instead of cry
You do not need to crave the world's attention
(I know... It would never be enough anyway)

I say to you in earnestness not mockery

That you can learn to love yourself

I hate clichés
But not as much as I hated feeling helpless
Unwanted
controlled
A puppet whose strings were mastered by a wine bottle and a single
thought playing in a regurgitated loop
"you're unloveable you're unloveable you're unloveable"

But I am on the other side now
mended in ways they told me was not possible
I am not the diagnosis that she gave me
or the one he gave or he gave or he gave

I stand here with scars you can barely see now
and students who say that I'm the light

I have witnessed the desperation that comes from thinking poetry
Is the only thing you have to drown the voices
And I know

That depression is not a placemat
and suicide is not a hump
and that 4 right turns will never equal progress
My genetics do not define me
(Let me say that one again)
MY GENETICS DO NOT DEFINE ME
and rape is just a four letter word that has no echo
I can fight back my addiction
I can take responsibility
and wipe the corners of my mouth without regretting all the things I did

I am anything but mediocre

And the lady on the corner?
is just selling roses
and if I see her
I will buy one
for you.

Future
The Lyrical Angel

I am Pinky and the Brain and I plan to take over the world!
Just kidding!
Tick, tock goes the clock, right on time…
Connecting the GPS…God's Positioning System to…
The spaceship that has returned to take me to my future.
Departing 2017, Destination eternity…
Passengers few, Layovers many!
Arriving…when the mission is completed!

Free
Taz Weysweete'

Running on a belly full of sky and shoveling in mouthfuls of reefer,
I seem to have forgotten that I am starving
Because I feel good
Bare feet on the boardwalk, my ears filled with stratosphere
I gave my last wish to a man playing the saxophone, flipped my penny into his hat.
He grinned at me and my dirty feet.
He grinned at my free.
It's cool
I can hear the stars.
So I grinned back.
Proceeded to kick up time and throw my soul in the tide.
Swam thru revival until my eyes became bloodshot testimony
If lightning strike me now, these bones will be heaven fried conviction
And my feet will be clean.

Crazy
Taz Weysweete'

For women who are called crazy when they're eyes were screaming I'm tired: part 1.

my child on my lap executing my right to bear arms. my man is screaming to let my child and the rifle, go.

but I'm fed up with letting go.
my son will not see me let go.
my daughter will not see me bend.

how many times was I let go?

left to defend my shade, my eye color, my hair, my history...alone?

even in this moment, I'm defending my mind, my heart, my home alone.

he better not call me no crazy bitch in front of my daughter.

I'm not crazy.

I haven't found the remedy to heal myself from the effects of the moon pounded into my soul
cannot control the way my eyelids concede to the rivers flowing from them, turning my poker face a Jim bean colored tattle tale, I'm trying to tell you, everything has been hurting for a long time
but it looks like I'm drunk and wanna fuck, looks like I wanna talk about revolution and war and the way the water moves
looks like I howl at the moon.
forever longing for that piece of me left hanging in the sky.
I read the confirmations, thru the phases.
in their faces
thru their words
or lack thereof
everything has meaning.
the hue in my eye matches that of my heart, I am the moons reflection in the summer time. yes, that was a chill you felt.

yes this is a gun.

I know exactly where I am in this moment.

don't call me crazy.

I said, For women who are called crazy when their eyes were screaming I'm tired

because Shange and Giovanni and Walker and Hurston are confined to blue line and Ink only read by those who know.

because Betty and Correta and Winnie and Camille are remembered as the wives of Kings instead of victims of progress

because you only know of Afeni and Assata because of Tupac and there is so much more to being a Shakur than being a man.

because Henrietta Lacks immortal cells are pressed into the genetic code of life don't tell me smoke ain't in my blood or that Madame C.J. Walker didn't die making sure that I felt patted my crown like royalty

because they will tell us later that they cremated Kathleen and Angela while each lobotomy is enjoyed by yet another scientist tampering with God..

say their Names! Korryn Gaines Sandra Bland and just like them

 I am not fucking crazy

but I point the shotgun towards my own head and pull the trigger everyday

because I play Russian Roulette with life or death every time I put a little blush on this Blackness

every time I stride with my head held high, my calf muscles exposed looking everything and nothing like the Black Stallion that courses through my veins

for the audacity to believe my Black life matters
and my children's Black Lives Matter and every King I have ever crossed
and have ever lost and that their Black Lives will always matter to me

because they will not pry away my loosie or my bullets.

because I will now and forever sip lemonade instead of tea

and I'm sorry

but ain't shit crazy about me.

The Aftermath
Brian Magill

The next day was work as usual.
The mood, quite somber.
Heavens clear of contrails for the next 3 days.
At a worship service a few days later
Could finally grieve.
Then, having no connection to the victims,
quietly moved on.

Watched in dismay as society succumbed
to the flickering memes.
The terror of phantom commandos.
Imagined supervillains lurking everywhere.
Yet no disruption to water or electricity.
Trash collected on time.
Neighborhoods as safe as the weeks before.

Didn't partake in the electronic Angel Dust.
Unwilling to listen to the purveyors of fear.
As usual played the straight man to another's nightmare.
Realized Cassandra's curse wasn't premonition,
Rather, stating the obvious to deaf ears.

Longed for the reassurance and vengeance of FDR.
Alas, our leaders were weak.
The chief of staff's nickname, "The Fart."
Far from a spare tire,
The V.P. wore the pants.

The Rule of Law forgotten,
At least for new arrivals and their kin.
Jailed first, charged months later.
A new Bermuda Triangle formed
Due south of Miami.

Instead of foes
Declared war on a nebulous thought.
Gave a rag tag band of brigands
the stature of Imperial Japan and the Nazis.
Thus began their excellent adventure.

No clear goals.
Just knocked heads together
And settled old scores.
No sacrifices at home.
Only request,
"Engage in a shopping spree."

The game went on for several years,
All financed on credit.
Fortunes pissed away.
Millions of lives destroyed,
Though few of our own.

Trashing countries is easier
Than governance.
Few cared what might emerge
from the wreckage in years to come.

Eventually the president brought down
Not by mortals,
But elementals and a bubble burst.
None the less,
Successor blamed for all that ensued
As he picked up the pieces.

Years have passed since that fateful day.
A collective amnesia has set in,
Though some injustices and paranoia live on.
Yet one can reject these narratives.
Follow the beat of your own drummer.
Mindful of immediate surroundings
And compassion for those far away.

Check Out My Bucket List
J. Scott Wilson

Well,
It happened today;
Today I didn't think of you once
That was the first time,
And it felt good
So good that
I think I'll not think of you tomorrow, twice

Maybe I'm finding myself,
But to do this finding
I had to get myself lost in you
Then I had to lose you,
And so
I've been lost in That for awhile
Until today,
And that was so good I think I'll do it tomorrow, twice

Maybe sometime I'll have a reunion
With myself,
But for now I'm just amazed at
How good it felt to not do something
I'll bet that reunion with myself will be
Pretty awesome, too,
But for now I'm going to revel in those moments
Of not thinking of you,
And I want to see how many of them I can accumulate
At one time
When I get enough of them together
I suppose I'll have to find something awesome
To fill them with
Like having an excess of buckets,
And discovering a Need to fill them

Watch me get excited to dream
Of what I can fill buckets with;
Buckets of Bones,
And Beach sand,
And Blood, and other Bodily Fluids
And Water and Beer and Women and Tomes of Poems and Pens I Killed

for art and Submissions to Magazines and Low Pay jobs, and
Whatever else I could
Fill these moments with.

It's
A dream of rebuilding
Reconditioning
Reuniting, and Re-   Living
Without reliving
Because I'm going to live for that Not Thinking About You
Tomorrow, twice

Back On The Road
Don Bent Spoke MacKellar

I was a Wreck When You Met Me,
But Now I'm Back On the Road
My Heart was Bent and Broken,
and I appreciate Being Towed

You've Hammered Everything Back Into Shape,
I'll Admit I was a little Nervous
Now You'll Always Be My Body Shop,
and I'm Crazy about your Parts and Service

There I was at the Side of the Road,
I was really Down on my Luck
But You Winked and Smiled with your Come Along
From the back of your Pickup Truck

I needed a Major Tune Up, and You were there for Me,
After all, as I recall, You Did the Job for Free
You've made all the right adjustments,
I'll Admit I was a little Nervous

Now You'll Always Be My Body Shop,
and I'm Crazy about your Parts and Service

You fixed the Gap in my Sparkplugs,
and lots of other things
But we both know there's still work to be done
(You've got me thinking about a Set of Rings)

I like the way you do your work,
I'll Admit I was a little Nervous
Now You'll Always Be My Body Shop,
and I'm Crazy about your Parts and Service

I was a Wreck When You Met Me,
But Now I'm Back On the Road
My Heart was Bent and Broken,
and I appreciate Being Towed

You've Hammered Everything Back Into Shape,

I'll Admit I was a little Nervous
Now You'll Always Be My Body Shop,
and I'm Crazy about your Parts and Service

Color Me Ready To Go
Don Bent Spoke MacKellar

I'd been down so far for so long
I had to look up to tie my shoe
My life had become monochromatic
everything in it was blue

I was ready by then to try something new
so I tried looking up
but the sky was blue and the wind
blew right through my coat too

My life could not have gotten much duller
so I began to look harder for another color

And I've finally developed a positive attitude
my outlook on life has been renewed
so now I'd have to say I think
my life is finally back in the pink

The Print of Van Gogh's Cypress Trees Hanging In My Therapist's Office
Nick Marickovich

I ask myself what Van Gogh,
Teeth stained with paint
Cheeks hollowed by syphilis
Breath reeking of coffee and liquor
Lonely, Unhinged, Sour,
Denied by even the cheap whores of Arles
The false joys of purchased pleasure;

What would he say now that
His turbulent trees, skies, grass
Rendered violently in deep gouges
Provide cold comfort to the splintered mind?
That from the fractured self
One might yet etch something beautiful
Into the transient night.

Why We Hide
Terry Cox-Joseph

Locked in bedroom closet—for a week!
Her whines and mews stretch
to the kitchen. Our legs pump
the stairs, follow wails

that bounce off walls, wend
through heat registers, sound
elusive as a ghost. We fling
open doors, drawers, closets.

Ah, there. She is safe.
It's her own fault. She loves
to hide in small spaces.
Can't help it. Just instinct.

Won't come out when we call.
Life goes on in a rush.
And when we leave,
we leave her without escape.

I used to be like that. Hiding
in closets, in attics. Away.
Anywhere. Alone. Instinct,
before I knew of meditation.

Difference was, I never forgave
when the door opened,
turned my back to cuddles.
Refused to purr with gratitude.

I've learned that others can open
doors. And I can open my own door.
Practice overcomes instinct.
Call and I may come.

Forgiveness, elusive as a ghost,
flings open closets, hides
in small spaces. Gratitude
purrs more easily with time.

The Makeover
Ann Falcone Shalaski

Silly me, standing
in front of my mirror, worried
that my sell-by date is past due,

longing to be someone else.
I think I'll bleach my hair,
stand life on its head.

Sit cross-legged in pink spandex thongs,
do yoga,
kick average,

add a little glitter. Dance topless
with silicone breasts bigger than beach balls.
Wear short black slips,

and kissee red lipstick.
I caught a glimpse of my reflection,
looked closer at the soft swell

of my body. The fine lines edged
with light – a woman ripened
like a sweet dark plum.

I liked what I saw.
I touched who I am.

Casablanca
Terrell K. Mercer

She told me my embrace was her escape
Shy eyes would barely meet mines before she would hide her face
I guess burying into my chest was like hiding from her woes
A peaceful silence drowning out the concerns of friends or foes
She gets a whiff of my fragrance ... then gently.... inhales
Her clutch tightens and in her touch I can feel the untold tales
She sighs a sigh that releases her burdens ....temporarily
I don't ask her what's wrong or is there anything to share with me
I just hold her and let her get lost...if only for these few moments that are
fleeting
And I imagine this isn't just physical ...I believe here our souls are meeting
Intertwining ...touching...agreeing ..seeking on the others behalf
This is where we share every intimate tear, heartache and laugh
Here is the timeless place where we share every unspoken word
This is the place where I will not let the world enter in to do her harm or
hurt
This is where our time meets eternity ...fixed point meets limbo
This is where love covers and judgment is thrown out the window
Here is our own personal corner of time and space
She seeks to escape but we are both found in our embrace

Burn
Star LaBranche

I was made of wood and he had matches

I stood next to him thinking I was basking
in his warmth
thinking everything he did was perfect
caring for my damaged wooden frame
when I had burned to the ground he
demanded I repair myself, because he
had more matches and he liked the way
I lit up

I was made of wood and another had matches

I did what he said because he had the matches
and told me they were my salvation
I hung on his every word because I knew
nothing and he had all the matches

there are still matches

but I'm different now; now I am made of stone

Sekhmet
Lisa Kendrick

Sekhmet, my savior, my mother:
though our lines were bred on separate planes,
and our lineage separated by time and space,
within us billows the same stardust,
our lungs the swell of event horizons,
our hearts the beat of fiery supernovas,
our skeletons the blossoming of nebulae.
We were the first to part the briny seas with our fingertips.
We will be the last to offer sanctuary beneath our shadows,
and when the curtains fall across the heavens,
we will be the last ones dancing.

Sekhmet, my goddess, my daughter:
what great creator made us?
We forged ourselves,
claws fired in raging furnaces,
fangs sharpened on scarred whetting stones,
hearts etched from ruddy lava flows,
eyes quarried in diamond mines,
spines sculpted from quarried granite,
hands wrapped in the silk of worms,
thighs draped with handspun velvet.
We are the breasts from which the starving suckle
We are the hips for which the passionate reach.
We are the arms that console desperate souls,
and when the scythe has left the fields naked,
we are the queens who will persevere.

Sekhmet, my liege, my sister:
goddesses fed us their milk for breakfast,
their ginger and raven hair swaying gently above our tiny fists,
their gilded arms teaching us magic,
weaving worlds before our eyes,
sewing nations together with their spirits,
birthing civilizations from their wombs.
We are creation.
We are destruction.
We are the alpha and the omega.
We are the world in one gulp,

power in one mighty swipe,
strength bristling with every thunderous stride.

Sekhmet, we are woman, we are sacred.

Natural Progression
David J.

He was a boy to whom the whole world seemed so bright, for the light within him had been dimmed by medication and correction.
He is a man to whom the world has grown so dim because his life has blinded him from the lightness of his being.

He was a boy who obsessed over the world of investigation and detective novels, hoping to someday solve the mystery of his own life.
He is a man who pursues the truth, examining every facet of a situation, and finding out only how much he still doesn't know.

He was a boy who sat on the sidelines, accepting of his status as the other and not the brother.
He is a man who has grown tired of accepting his fate and boldly stumbles through existence trying to reclaim what was lost.

He was a boy who bought the dream of a bright future if he just had the faith.
He is a man who lives in the nightmare of broken promises that never came true.

He was a boy who was fiercely loved by a few, but always sought to have more.
He is a man who has grown weary of fickle people and only wants the devotion of a few.

He was a boy who wanted for nothing, except the physical touch of one who loved him out of a conscious choice and not just familial obligation.
He is a man who fears to touch another for fear of their revulsion at his overpowering craving for affection.

He was a teenager who hedged his bets in love, fearing rejection over lack of affection, holding out for a sure thing.
He has become a man who regrets not learning from the mistakes he feared to make, knowing so little of love for the lack of ventures pursued.

He was a boy who excelled at academics, but failed at interaction.
He was a teen who traded his brilliance for practicality, normalcy and acceptance.
He became a young man blindly chasing a profession he would grow to

detest, only to reject it, start again and repeat the cycle in another field.
He is now a man who is dredging the depths of the murky waters to salvage
the remnants of the dream that once gave him feeling and made him feel
alive. But time has cast a rime of patina upon the chambers of his heart
and a blight of rust upon the creativity of his minds.

He was a boy with no past who became a man without a future.
He lives all day longing for the past he can't change, he spends his nights in
terror of a future he could alter if only he was stronger.
Once able to create entire fantastical landscapes out of thin air, the only
images that readily spring to mind now are images that are far too real and
bleak.
He has spent too many years trying to recapture the boy, that he has made
an empty husk of the man.

He has obsessed over the past and feared the future for so long that he
never learned to be PRESENT! And the only gift he has left is stirring the
waters, hoping to find some clarity. But the more he stirs things up, the
cloudier they become. Once a victim of tunnel vision, he now has a
panoramic view so broad that he cannot focus or determine depth or
perspective of any object.

As a child, he was always silenced and subdued.
As a man, he has lost his voice and now has only two settings: mumble and
shout.

But there is another in the room, in his head, in his heart.
This persona says to let the child go and DAMN THE MAN!

And like a butterfly, he emerges.
Changed in every way so as to be unrecognizable from the former.
Today is the day he takes back his life, free from the shackles of the past
and unafraid of the future ahead.

He is hungry for a challenge, but always seeks balance.
He knows his limits and instead of lamenting them, EMBRACES them and
then pushes them further.
He is fearless and brave.
He used to wear confidence like a mask, now it is his crown.
He has taken the blanket of his insecurities and he has put it behind his
shoulders like a child pretending to be a caped superhero.
He has taken the lemons thrown at him, added the sweetness of his heart,
cast them into the fire and created hard candy, equal parts joy and sorrow.

Now he has distributed them to the masses as a testament to his victory over himself.

He no longer fears transparency because no one can hurt him as much as he has already hurt himself and refuses to go back to that place.
He has finally learned to temper his honesty with tact and knows that it's often by pushing through the darkness that you finally see the light.

He is still the boy.
He has become a man.
He has the heart of the young and the wisdom of the aged.

The lantern within him has grown so bright that now he is a lighthouse to those who seek shelter and safety.
Forward he surges on uncharted waters, ready for adventure and wherever the winds will take him

Scars On My Soul
Victoria Cartagena

I wonder if these scars will stick to my soul...
Will they grow as I grow?
I wonder if these scars are like permanent tattoos
never really considered them taboo.
I wonder if these scars are now a part of me
Can they speak my story for me?
I wonder if these scars are here to stay
I don't know if I want them to go away.
I wonder if ...
They will leave me stamped
Like an expired produce food that nobody wants
Or maybe they will make me exclusive, special edition
who am I kidding...
I wonder if my screams can be heard?
Herd?
No not like a flock ... more like a block
A stop
A please
A plead
A scream
....
Some one!! Can you hear me?
Near?
No far please ... please stay far these scars are so deep!
I wonder if these scars will stick to my soul ...
So when I go home He can heal them.
Please don't take them away
They are comforting me ... they tell my story.
My scars ... my scars ... they are me.

What The Sycamore Saw
(Based on Luke 19:1-10)
Judith Stevens

I stand the ancient city near Jordan, called Jericho,
    a sycamore tree, growing north of the Dead Sea,
      eight hundred feet below sea level.

(Though really a fig mulberry, with little valued fruit,
      one day I bore a man.)
    My rustling leaves first brought news -
everyone spoke of the coming teacher - so unlike the others
    I leaned closer, the better to hear,
  my roots, thick and spreading, owning the road,
my girth, large: three people around might encircle me.

I am a sturdy tree, grown tall and spread with large flat leaves.
    My low limbs invite climbing.
When this Jesus visited our town, people were curious -
    thronging the road, jostling for a closer look.
      (His face, the kindest I had ever seen.)

A diminutive man ran in front of the crowd,
      jockeying for position where Jesus would pass.
Small in stature - pushed aside, carried along on outskirts,
    so short, he strained to see over,
dressed in expensive brocades, I recognized him at once.
    Everyone knew him - Jericho's chief tax collector -
      (quite wealthy - though no friends).
Rumor whispered he raised taxes - kept part for himself.
      (People avoided him.)

The first surprise! Zacchaeus clambered into my branches for a better view,
      began climbing.
Now the crowd surged around me - stopped - as Jesus looked up
    beneath exact spot where Zacchaeus perched.
  This Jesus locked eyes with the rich man, said clearly,
"Zacchaeus, come down; I mean to stay at your house today."

Suddenly so still you could have heard my leaves rustle
    like a beating heart: (crowd murmuring in disbelief,

"He means to stay in the sinner's house while here are upstanding
citizens?")

I felt Zacchaeus hasten down - a human squirrel.
    He welcomed the Teacher reverently, with great joy.
(Some said the man who came down from my branches
    looked nothing at all like the one who went up, so altered was he.)

        Zacchaeus turned to Jesus,faced his accusers.
His new voice rang out: "Today, half of my wealth l give to the poor.
If I have defrauded anyone in the least, him I will pay back four-fold."

        Jesus smiled,turned to the crowd, spoke softly,
"Behold,the Son of Man came to seek and to save that which was lost.
        Now is salvation come to this house."
The last thing I saw - the two of them together,heads bent,talking,
    walking down the road, followed by curious townsfolk.

Many years have passed. I've puzzled   repeatedly - still no answer for
what I saw.
    (Towns people called it a "miracle" - he gave back money he stole,
four-fold,
        and stole no more.)
    Did Zacchaeus truly find salvation - redemption? (such important
sounded words)

        I cannot say.
    I am only a sycamore.   But I know what I saw.

    Jesus transformed a tax collector and an entire town
        with love - without judging.
By focusing on the good in that small man's heart,
    he called forth justice from Zacchaeus,
and helped him, for the first time, live up to the meaning of his name.*

(Zacchaeus: Greek from Hebrew – cleansed, purified, righteous, just)

Dear Woman
BlackRoyalty

"I hope one day the moonlight reflects off your tear drops and make you sparkle..

I hope one day you find a man strong enough to bathe in your sorrows…

I hope tomorrow..
If not this evening....
that your strength replace your weakness..
As if you got a face lift to make your smile permanent..

Let your crying become your own personal baptism..
Stop letting your pain linger
and let those tears become your cleanser....

And remember…
You must first love yourself
before trying to love somebody else…
Don't eat the poison that's being feed to you…
Be the chef....
Dear woman"

Pushing Limits
Maddie Garcia

The mind is constantly risking absurdity
Pushing the limits
And some of us end up believing it

A body of energy attracting energy
Without filter
Accepting distortion being fed

Accumulating in a mental garbage-can
Causing an overflow
Eventually,
Throwing up words
that the body reabsorbs

Getting sucked into the skin
Sinking, into your dermis
Fighting to scratch them off
To prevent from getting into your blood

You believe
Because the mind is a very powerful thing

Reality is taking one step at a time
Not swimming into a pool of lies
Walking before you run
Setting small goals to achieve all that's possible

Don't become the joke
But learn to laugh at yourself
The mind becomes irrational
Only if you allow it

Don't fall for the charade
Love comes from within
Becoming an extension of yourself
So the love you express to others
People must see in you first

Mind games

Those are nonsense
Remember a king without a queen
Is checkmate

Find the source
The higher power that is within all
Because when the mind gets out of control
That should be our safe zone

Don't be so open
That you fall through the cracks
But limit yourself

Make the gaps smaller
In case you stumble
There is enough ground
To catch yourself

The mind is a balance
That may tilt both ways
Don't become a parody
Be your best original self

Don't believe absurdity
Force the scale the other way
A mind on the loose can be your worst enemy
A mind under control is your best friend

The Mirror
Tanya Deloatch

It told on me
And I quickly looked back
Wondering who was that person
And where was I at?!
Years had gone by
And youth had long faded
Yet it was clearly visible
When the mirror caught me jaded
Stress was no friend of mine
Illness either
And the mirror had joined in
Becoming a deceiver
Of the appearance I expected to see that day
But youth had long faded
And age gave me away
☐

When I glanced back
The truth set in
I was more than an image
Of way back when
Educated and wise
Well beyond those years
When I fought through experiences
And faced my fears
Raised all of my children to be a success
So how dare I feel like a defeated mess?!
My outer appearance was as fine as a perfectly aged wine
And by no mirror, illness or stress
Would I be defined
So the eyes in the mirror
Did not reflect negativity
But in truth
Showed the best parts of all of me....

And The Award Goes To
Raymond Simmons

Girl you should have won the Oscar
For your skill at playing your part.
Your sound routine in every scene
Was played so well you broke my heart.

You knew what made me laugh, and sigh.
You pretended we were perfect.
And in the end you made me cry.
You really knew how to worked it.

Your great performance accented,
Every dramatic scene you tried.
With talent well represented
You took me along for the ride.

I never heard anyone yell
For lights, or camera, or action,
Yet every scene was played so well
And you beamed with satisfaction.

You were director, star, and crew,
And every scene became your own,
And my eyes were focused on you,
In spite of foul moods, grunts, and groans.

Though sometimes numb from weariness,
I Faithfully carried your gear.
I believed it was for the best
Because it eased your deepest fear

You threw up so many defenses
I didn't see the plot get thicker
And when I came to my senses
I was locked out of the picture.

I was just a prop, killing time,
It took a while to understand,
That I was never on your mind,
And never in your future plan.

Clear thoughts erase those once confused.
My once blind eyes now opened wide.
I see now what the camera views
I know now what you've tried to hide.

We never got to settle this,
Your movie I never did see.
You yelled wrap and I was dismissed.
That's cool, I hated your movie.

From the start this was your project
To the end you are the subject.
There can be no doubt in my mind
That your name will grace every line.

For sure you'll take all the credit,
And be thoroughly self-vaunting.
So you just watch, view and edit.
It's the award you've been wanting.

Noticed
Bboy Cabi

Queen, the biggest thing about you is your smile,

You carry so much light in such a fun-sized slice of heaven

I can scarcely imagine why anyone who ever got close

Would ever search for another smile

You carry your crown like its fly
you wear your joy so plainly
you are beautiful

the brightness of the jewels you carry
can attract attention, be wary
it's not your fault,
it's just even losers can recognize legendary

They confuse love for possession
so they try to own your image
and trap your light in the limits of their expectations

They can't handle the shine
 so they try to make you tone it down

They don't see the steel sheathed beneath your softness

You're real sharp

The unexpected cut of your confidence
carves through the facade they try to smother you with

There is no cage that can hold your light

Up Daniel's Hill
Jack Callan

Couldn't get up the hill in my truck,
    so I borrowed his beater-Jeep
  to climb the long mud-slick driveway.
Could just reach the pedals,
    didn't adjust the seat.
        (I'd done it before the rains.)
Got 'er warmed up, down the hill
    while I loaded in my stuff -
  slow goin' and' I barely reached the gas -
    two tires low, planning to fill 'em on top.

So up through the gate I went,
    slowin' to dip into crooked rain ditches,
        cut on angles to catch the flow,
lurchin' the Jeep from side to side,
    bouncin' and spinnin', gettin' uphill somehow.
        Got to the steep mud, started slowin' down.

Knew I would not make it up - had no choice -
    I'd have to back it down.
So in reverse I go - break pedaled to the floor -
    I pushed it all the way down. Wouldn't go no more.
Needed to go slow, lookin' my shoulder, huggin' the seat.
    The mud-spattered rear window
      showed a grisly scene:
ruts not too deep, loose rocks, sides slicked smooth -
        a long way down.
Brake floored, I tried to steer straight.
    The Jeep wanted sideways - kept sliding' to the edge.
Nothin' I did would stop my descent down the side of the hill.
    I knew it was over.
So I faced straight, slid under the wheel, pushed down the brake
    with both feet, hard as I could.
This green city boy jes' kep' slidin' -
    couldn't see a thing from the floorboard.
    Flashin' thoughts: friend's car, battered body,
      what my wife would say.

Then Silence. The car just stopped,

back wheels at the edge of the rim.
Without takin' a breath, I grabbed my phone,
            still under the wheel -
    called my friend: "You on top?" I asked 'im.
He laughed and said he heard me comin, then stop.
            "What happened?"
Still laughin', he told me how to put it in four-wheel-drive
        and shift it the moment it caught.
                Still squeezin' the brake, I did.
    Sat up, put it in drive, hit the gas and hoped to God

On the very edge, the tires caught - lurched forward,
    back tires loosenin' gravel and dirt.
But up I went, slidin' right and left, fast and furious,
    up, up to the house and my laughin' friend,
        me more than wide awake.

    I got out, laughin' too;
            there we were, like nothin' happened
                And nothin' did.

Dig
Tanya Cunningham

I started digging with a plastic spoon
turning and shifting soft earth looking for
the moon.

First, I found the half me, the past me, the
girl with the dirty nails who used to have
me.

But, she was undone. Less than one.
So, I wrapped her in love coils.
Closed her eyes with my fingers, but her back in the soil.

And my favorite seed, became my favorite tree.
Watered with brown tears, the leaves became
my favorite me.

My trunk made of whispered prophecies
spoken in cafés by the suns of Pharisees.

Grown strong.
Soul long.

My soul longed to define my second birth
to push my roots deeper and touch the hidden earth.
Find life past six feet and dwell in the dirt.

Become the search. Not the seeker.
Giver. Not the reaper.
Teacher of saplings.
"The light's this way. Want sun? Get at me.
Go left. Left again. And you could circle the world.
No worries, the trail's marked with pine needles and rock pearls.
See the girl – grown bigger than men.
Hair like canopies, arms like limbs.
And a taste of my flesh could be your first sin.
Enjoy the shade.
Take a bite.
Begin again.

This collection has attempted to represent the journey of all man. More importantly, it is meant to support those who are still in the midst of their trials and searching for their resurrection. Accordingly, all proceeds will go to G.R.O.W. Foundation.

G.R.O.W. Foundation, Inc. is a non-profit organization connecting women affected by domestic violence with the resources needed to lead a safe and productive life. It is G.R.O.W.'s unwavering goal to empower these women with the tools needed to become financially independent and self-sufficient.

For more information on G.R.O.W. or to donate, please visit growfoundationva.org.

If you or someone you know is affected by domestic violence and in need of emergency shelter, please call, the National Domestic Hotline at 1-800-799-7233.

Evolutions

Made in the USA
Middletown, DE
18 March 2017